TIGER-SHOOTING IN INDIA

TIGER-SHOOTING IN INDIA;

BEING AN ACCOUNT OF

HUNTING EXPERIENCES ON FOOT IN RAJPOOTANA,

DURING THE HOT SEASONS,

FROM 1850 TO 1854

WILLIAM RICE

GYAN

Published by

Gyan Publishing House
5, Ansari Road
Daryaganj, New Delhi-110002
Phone: 011-47034999, 9811692060
E-mail: books@gyanbooks.com

Distribution Network
gyanbooks.com
India, USA, Canada, UK, Australia

ISBN: 978-93-6433-011-4 (PB)
First Published, 1857

2nd Impression 2024

Printed at: Gyan Press, Delhi.

TIGER-SHOOTING IN INDIA
Author: WILLIAM RICE

TIGER-SHOOTING IN INDIA;

BEING AN ACCOUNT OF

HUNTING EXPERIENCES ON FOOT

IN RAJPOOTANA,

DURING THE HOT SEASONS,

FROM 1850 TO 1854.

BY

WILLIAM RICE,

LIEUTENANT 25TH REGIMENT BOMBAY N. I., AND LATE CAPTAIN
TURKISH CONTINGENT.

WITH TWELVE PLATES IN CHROMALITHOGRAPHY,
FROM SKETCHES BY THE AUTHOR.

LONDON:
SMITH, ELDER AND CO., 65, CORNHILL.
BOMBAY: SMITH, TAYLOR AND CO.

1857.

TO

COLONEL JOHN JACKSON, C.B.,

LATE COMMANDING THE 25TH REGIMENT BOMBAY NATIVE INFANTRY,

THESE PAGES ARE INSCRIBED

AS A

SLIGHT TOKEN OF RESPECT AND REGARD

BY HIS OBLIGED FRIEND

THE AUTHOR.

PREFACE.

My object in writing these pages is to give, to the best of my humble abilities, some account of the most exciting and glorious sport this world affords—Tiger-shooting; believing that it is a subject which excites general interest, and as to which a pretty considerable amount of ignorance exists, even in India. I also wish to point out how very inefficient the very best weapons now used by the tiger-hunter are for the purpose. This may seem presumption on my part, as I can say little or nothing of the usual method employed in India for killing tigers. Once only was it my lot to assist at the death of a tiger, from the back of an elephant. That was my first introduction to the sport, and very likely would have been my last, had I—as doubtless very many others have done—supposed that an elephant was absolutely necessary to enable one to take the field against tigers.

During several expeditions in pursuit of "large game," under which comprehensive title the Indian sportsman includes lions, tigers, panthers, bears, elephants, bison, &c., I enjoyed many splendid opportunities of observing the habits of these animals, and ascertaining how they may best be killed; therefore I cannot do better than attempt to describe what has actually come under my own observation, leaving the reader to judge of the value of my testimony.

The following pages have been compiled from my journal, which was regularly kept at the conclusion of each day's hunting, giving an account of the sport shared by certain friends and myself during several intervals of "leave of absence," obtained for the express purpose of Tiger-shooting. Our expeditions extended over a space of nearly five years, but they occupied in the aggregate just 365 days of actual sport.

Here it may be as well to explain to the uninitiated, that in India it is almost hopeless to attempt hunting wild beasts, with any reasonable chance of success, except during the three hottest months in each year. The best part of these seasons, during nearly five years, was, therefore, selected by us for our several sporting expeditions. The heavy rains that generally commence at the end of June, and last, with slight intermissions, for the next four months, by completely swamping the whole country, preclude all idea of hunting. The dense foliage and grass that everywhere spring up, and last for the succeeding five months, prevent all progress through the vast forests and jungles; not to mention the extreme unhealthiness, even to natives, of all uncleared and uncultivated districts at this time of the year. The remaining three months, or "hot season," is therefore the best and only time left for tiger-hunting. Then the great scarcity of water, the comparatively open appearance of the country, and the intense heat, which drives the beasts during the daytime to the shadiest and most secluded retreats, are all so many chances in favour of the sportsman.

Considerable preparations have to be made, before one or more hunters, supposing they have not the valuable assistance of elephants, can set out to kill a tiger. In the first place, each man has to supply himself with three or more double guns, or rifles. To carry these into the field, at least two natives are required to each sportsman. In the steadiness of these men you must have perfect confidence, for it is their duty to quickly hand you the spare loaded guns; the one you have just discharged at the infuriated beast being thrown down anywhere, in the hurry consequent on these occasions (often to its no small detriment). No matter how near or unexpectedly the game may be come upon, or how great their numbers may be, or what amount of roaring they may indulge in—nothing must for a moment disconcert these gun-carriers, otherwise the hunter on foot will most likely find himself in an awkward predicament.

Here let me stop to pay a just tribute to the extraordinary courage and nerve constantly displayed in the most trying and alarming situations by the "Shikarees," as the natives are called who are employed, on account of their knowledge of the animal's habits, to assist in finding the game, and who accompany their masters at the time of its being killed. Rarely, indeed, does a panic occur among these men; although themselves unarmed, and mostly unable to use our guns, they cheerfully and coolly venture into the most perilous places; exhibiting an amount of courage and composure all the while, that I firmly believe no European, not personally engaged in the exciting conflict, could possibly even equal. Still, human nature is not infallible, and temporary panics will, and do sometimes occur; how, nobody ever knows, but quite as often originating with the hunters themselves, as with their followers. Where then are the requisite spare loaded guns? Out of sight, perhaps; the bearer having either precipitately betaken himself to flight, or nimbly gained the topmost branch of the nearest tree, flinging down the gun anywhere in his panic. A pleasant position this for the sportsman, and one which nothing but some wonderfully lucky chance prevents from ending with a catastrophe.

Suppose, in another case, all the guns being empty, the wounded beast makes off, followed by the excited and completely blown hunter; who, in vain, attempts to reload even one gun, in time to overtake the flying game! Again, it may be asked—although I never once knew an instance of a "Shikaree" ever hesitating or refusing to follow anywhere after a wild beast, whether wounded or not—is it exactly fair to require these men to risk so much, seeing that they have but so very small a temptation in the shape of reward or profit? for, to consider such work sport to them, is quite out of question.

Besides the inconvenience of having so many guns to carry (with fewer it would be mere folly to attack large game) there is no small risk incurred to all parties by carelessness or inquisitiveness on the part of those to whom the guns are temporarily entrusted. Several times I have known a gun to have been accidentally fired off most unpleasantly close to the sportsman; and to receive one already full cocked from the hands of a gun-carrier is a very common occurrence indeed: the said gun having been probably so carried for miles through dense bushes; placing, no doubt, at times, the life of some one of the party in jeopardy.

But, perhaps, the crowning evil is the chance of losing your guns altogether (generally averaging in value £40 each) by the want of honesty of those into whose charge they have been given. It frequently happens that you may never before have seen these men; but, from the necessity of changing the bearers as each fresh part of the country has to be hunted over, one is compelled to place this blind confidence in every man's honesty. Rarely indeed is this trust abused; still, I once did lose three valuable rifles in this manner: but this is far too unpleasant a subject to dwell upon.

Again, the nature of the ground frequently obliges the hunter to climb some tree, or high bank, before a shot can be obtained at the game; covers often being so dense that no animal could be seen moving through them, even at a distance of merely three or four yards around: moreover, tigers are often found lying out in some wide open space, where the grass is high over a man's head, and a view can only be had from some tree. In such cases, besides the trouble and peril of handing up and down so many loaded guns, much valuable time is lost; and the beast, perhaps, passes out of shot before the spare gun can be got ready. All this vexatious delay would be avoided, if only one gun were used, which would never have to leave the sportsman's hands.

Another annoyance consequent on the number of guns, often happens to the tired hunter. Occasionally sudden and heavy showers of rain, even during the "hot season," come on; he then has the treat of thoroughly cleaning some four or five double guns: an operation he hardly dare trust to his servants, lest by their carelessly neglecting to dry the guns well, serious consequences might ensue from a miss-fire, on his next meeting with any fierce animal. This cleaning performance is really no joke, especially if it has to be repeated for several days together (as I have known to be the case in a wet "hot season") before the field can be taken at all. It is quite impossible to prevent so many guns getting wet; whereas, perhaps, one only, with care, might be kept dry. Another drawback is, that so many guns lead to great expense; for nobody would trust his life with any but really good ones. The "hot season," or time for big game shooting being over, for the remaining nine months of the year the sportsman can have no use for more than one gun at a time; the rest lie idle; and, besides requiring much looking after to prevent rusting, are rather weighty baggage to travel with.

Having regard to these little inconveniences, it follows that the best description of gun or rifle is a repeating one; which the hunter, by always himself carrying, ever finds ready to his hand. No spare gun is then required; no accidental discharges occur; you have no bother when in trees or climbing high rocks; no occasion to trust your property to any doubtful characters; no need to risk for your own amusement any one else's life; no expensive "battery" to keep up, nor any waste of time and labour in keeping the same clean and fit for work.

So convinced was I of these facts, that more than four years ago (when the then newly-invented repeating fire-arms first appeared, and greatly raised the hopes of hunters) I caused two revolving rifles, of five shots each, to be sent out to me from England, expressly for large game shooting. Without the slightest wish to decry anybody's inventions, I must say, that more miserable weapons for this purpose could scarcely be imagined. Dearly might I have paid for making my first experiment with them on a stout old tiger. The bullets seemed to have no penetrating power whatever, on such a mass of sinew, muscle, and bone; none had gone in more than six inches deep: which fact I discovered on skinning the brute, after having killed him with my usual double rifle (a Westley Richards, of No. 18 bore). The shots from these revolvers could have merely "tickled" the tiger; as the natives present generally remarked. This want of force, doubtless, arises from the great escape of gunpowder, at the moment of discharge, from both ends of the barrel; which, besides burning the left arm in the attempt to steady the rifle, by as usual grasping the barrel, creates such a smoke that the sight of the rifle, as well as the beast fired at, are both obscured for some little time, should there unluckily be no high wind to clear off the smoke at once. These revolvers, at short distances, with a rest to steady them, would, perhaps, kill small deer well enough, but certainly not any sort of large game. I am still convinced, however, that a repeating rifle is the proper arm for the Indian hunter; but very material improvements in construction and manufacture are required to render this description of gun effective.

In conclusion, I can only say that I earnestly desire to be allowed the opportunity of proving the powers of the rifle on the numerous tigers that infest the island of Singapore. The fearful ravages committed by these pests, and the daily loss of life inflicted on the native population in the immediate vicinity of the town of Singapore itself, are notorious evils, which have long required a remedy. Notwithstanding that the reward or price set upon each tiger's head has been greatly increased by the Indian Government in the last year or so, still I have been truly informed that it acts but as a very slight check indeed to the depredations constantly carried on by these ferocious beasts of prey. This is owing to the danger and difficulty of waging any effectual sort of warfare against these plagues, on account of there being no trained elephants procurable on the island at present. Elephants in a wild state are numerous enough in the forests on the opposite coast, but hitherto no trained ones have, I believe, been shipped to Singapore. Consequently, in the absence of the assistance of these valuable animals, the local sportsmen, wisely enough, decline the unequal contest: at least to any great extent. The tigers can, therefore, commit any havoc, almost with impunity.

There the old notion prevails, that without elephants, tigers are best let alone. Now, I have not the faintest intention of wishing for an instant to under-rate the efforts of others, and I am wholly unable to give an opinion (never having had the good fortune to visit the island) as to the practicability of making any sort of impression on the tigers of Singapore. Very many difficulties might render the task almost impossible; such as the unfavourable nature of the ground, the density of the covers and swamps, or the impenetrable nature and vast extent of the jungle in which these beasts may have their retreats: also, perhaps, the apathy or fear of the natives, who, from superstitious motives, might be unwilling to render any assistance. Still, at the risk of being considered merely an idle boaster, I cannot but feel that an attempt to exterminate such brutes should be made on the score of humanity; and I here beg leave to offer my services for the work.

Having the honour to belong to the Bombay army, I am well aware that, to obtain the necessary leave to enable me to reach Singapore, and return thence after each hunting season, would be far too much to expect, especially at this crisis; moreover, it might appear, in the eyes of the authorities, very like an attempt to shirk my regimental duty, in order to gratify my passion for tiger-hunting; I, therefore, most respectfully beg that my honourable masters, should they approve the cause, may see fit to attach me temporarily to some Madras regiment, doing duty either at Singapore or some of the neighbouring stations in Burmah. This would at least enable me to make an experiment on these Singapore tigers; and one season would prove whether they could be mastered or not. In return for so great a boon, I can only pledge myself to offer the beasts either of these agreeable alternatives: they shall have frequent chances of either "eating my bullets," as "Blackey" says, or myself! If even but a few tigers were killed in one particular spot, the natives themselves would, doubtless, be able to prevent their re-appearance; for this has ever been the case, according to my knowledge, in many places in India, where tigers formerly abounded. But at the worst, to fail in such a cause would be no disgrace. All I ask is to be allowed to make the experiment, either at Singapore, or any other part of India infested by wild beasts: wherever tigers prove troublesome, it would be equally agreeable to me, so long as there was a chance of plenty of sport, and the painful doubt was removed of being able to obtain "leave of absence" for the purpose.

Being well aware that, in England, the narratives of any one who is rash enough to relate Indian Sporting Adventures, even of the very mildest description, are apt to be received by his audience with doubt or ridicule, if not with positive incredulity, I have thought it advisable to append the following list of "witnesses," who will gladly corroborate, as far as they are individually concerned, every statement contained in this Journal:—

A. B. Little, Lieut. and Adjutant 25th Regiment Bombay Native Infantry.

F. A. Loch, Lieut. and Adjutant 1st Bombay Light Cavalry, Lancers.

R. G. Lord, Dr. 21st Regiment Bombay Native Infantry.

H. E. Forbes, Lieut. 1st Regiment Bombay, Lancers.

H. H. Elliot, Lieut. 1st Regiment Bombay, Lancers, Aide-de-Camp to Lord Elphinstone, Governor of Bombay.

D. Gaye, Captain Bombay Artillery.

J. H. B. Hallen, Esq., 1st Light Cavalry, Lancers, Bombay.

During the year's sport in Rajpootana, India, our "bag" consisted of 156 head of "large game," killed and wounded, as follows:—68 tigers killed, 30 wounded, total 98. Panthers killed 3, wounded 4, total 7. Bears killed 25, wounded 26, total 51.*

* Several others of the above-named animals are confidently supposed to have been wounded, but they are not included in the list, as no blood could be found to clearly prove the fact: this was our invariable test, but by no means always a correct one.

CONTENTS.

CHAPTER VI.

CHAPTER VII.

CHAPTER VIII.

CHAPTER IX.

CHAPTER X.

CHAPTER XI.

Chapter XII.

Chapter XIII.

Chapter XIV.

Chapter XV.

Chapter XVI.

Chapter XVII.

LIST OF PLATES.

TIGER-SHOOTING IN INDIA.

CHAPTER I.

My first attempt—Its results on myself—Get a month's leave—First kill—How to make bears' grease—The Bheels—"Wull"—First tiger.

The 25th Regiment Bombay Native Infantry marched from camp Malligaum, Kandeish, and relieved the 33rd Bengal Native Infantry, stationed at camp Neemuch, Rajpootana, on the 14th February, 1850. This brought me within reach of a hunting ground abounding in large game. One month afterward I made a first attempt to bag a "royal Bengal tiger."

Having heard that there was a tiger at a village named "Bahara," thirteen miles west of camp, my brother officer, Lieutenant Little, and myself, rode out there in the morning, having sent on our guns over night by our servants. We collected about twenty men from the village, and proceeded to beat several very likely looking covers in the neighbourhood in search of this tiger. But, although in several places we saw his foot-prints quite fresh, he could nowhere be found. My friend was obliged to ride back to camp in the evening, but I determined to stop in the hope of getting a shot at this tiger by moonlight, having been assured by the natives that the beast invariably came down to drink every night at a tank, or large piece of water, close to their village. As a bait for the tiger, I tied up by the horns a poor lame half-starved bullock to a tree stump, and afterwards climbed up a small tamarind-tree close by. Here I seated myself with three double guns on some boughs we had cut and placed crosswise in the tree, and silently awaited the tiger's coming. After watching for about three or four hours the moon went down. It now became too dark to distinctly see any mark, so I let down my three guns to the foot of the tree, and prepared to descend myself. No sooner had my feet touched the ground, than an appalling roar from a thick bush, not a dozen paces off, caused me to almost jump out of my skin. I instantly seized a gun, and blazed away at random both barrels into the bush, in the hope that my enemy would take the hint and disperse. To my horror he only repeated the roar still louder. In the fright consequent thereon, and not being able to see the tiger, or well knowing what I was about, I banged off the remaining guns into the bush. Each of these shots was answered by more roars. Having no other loaded guns left, I ran off at a marvellous pace towards the village. Here, to my great joy, I met some men hastening towards me. They, it appeared, had been waiting to hear my shot from the tree, which should announce the tiger's death; but seeing from the flashes of my guns that I was on the ground, and hearing the repeated shots and loud roaring, concluded that I had chosen to fight the tiger on foot, and had of course killed him. After undeceiving them, they volunteered to accompany me back to the tree to recover the guns I had left behind in my flight, as well as to release the bullock.

Just as we had picked up the unloaded guns we were saluted by another roar close by, which caused us all to hastily retreat, leaving the unfortunate bullock still tied up. I had observed some time before getting down from the tree that the bullock made fearful struggles to get loose. Doubtless he smelt the tiger; but I concluded that he was like myself, merely tired of waiting so long in one place. After passing the rest of the night under a large tree, where my horse and man were waiting, I went at dawn to look for the bullock, but found the poor beast killed and half eaten. I was obliged to be back in camp early that morning, or might have had a good chance of finding the tiger lying asleep somewhere near, after having so gorged himself. As it was, there was no time left to look for him; and having well paid the owner of the dead bullock, I rode back to camp, much begrudging the tiger the dinner of beef he had so fairly won at my expense; and making a vow never to be again guilty of such slow unsportsman-like work as watching in ambush at night for any wild beast. This tiger must somehow have been aware of my presence in the tree, and have merely roared to get rid of me that he might dine at leisure. None of my shots, luckily, could have touched him, or perhaps, being enraged, he would not have let me escape so easily.

Such was my first adventure with the tiger. The hot weather having now fairly set in, I obtained a month's leave, from 26th March to 26th April, 1850. Before starting on my hunting expedition, having heard that the country was in rather a disturbed state, and the people not over friendly or obliging to white strangers, I was advised to apply to the political authorities for the province of Meywar for "purwannahs," or papers authorizing me to travel about in the neighbouring districts, as well as to enable me more easily to procure supplies. This sort of passport was refused me on the ground that I might become embroiled with the natives. So I at once started without these valuable documents for "Ruttunghur," a fortress 32 miles to the north-east of our camp, intending to hunt eastward along a range of hills. My two camels being completely done up with such a long first march, we did not reach our ground till midnight. I slept out under a tree, and was next morning awoke by Lieut. H. R——, Bombay Engineers, who was engaged in surveying the surrounding country. He kindly invited me to put up for the day at his tent, which enabled me to send on my kit or baggage six miles along the hills, to the village of Lohareea. I gave directions for some men to be collected, intending to hunt there next morning, for the country looked very likely ground for bears. H. R—— was slightly lame, having been lately wounded by an arrow fired at him by some Bheels, while he was trying to stop a disturbance that had arisen between them and some of his followers. In the evening I returned to my tent, and the next morning set out with about twenty men for the hills. Here I soon found a large male bear, which I luckily killed with the first shot in the head, rather to the astonishment of the men with me. Being not very far from the tent, we carried him there on poles, took off his skin, and pegged it down.

I tried to make some bears' grease, having promised to bring back some to friends in camp, if lucky in my sport; but the fat soon got putrid and covered with ants and insects; moreover, the crows, kites, and village dogs walked off with it; no place being safe from them.

It was long before we found out the proper way to preserve the grease, which is as follows:—Cut off the fat in long strips, and with sticks poke these into empty bottles; when filled, cork down the bottles, and place them all day in the sun. The fat soon melts, and now looks like oil; but when it cools again at night, becomes quite firm and white, without any offensive smell whatever. Capital stuff for cleaning guns, for it never rusts; moreover, scented with bergamot, &c., it is much prized by "exquisites" for the hair. In this way we yearly concocted great quantities of both bear and tiger fat, the latter being considered by natives as an infallible cure for rheumatism.

After my first kill, I passed some days in hunting from place to place, finding some bears, but no tigers. I had the luck to kill four bears, between the 28th March and 3rd April. My men were Bheels, a race I cannot better describe than by comparing them to the "Santhals"—a name now pretty familiar to the English public, from the late rebellion in Bengal. From constantly living in the woods, these men are all well acquainted with the habits of every description of animals to be found there, and are consequently first-rate hunters—they are brave even to rashness, and capable of enduring any amount of fatigue. They mostly carry a small axe, bow and arrows, or short spear, with perhaps a leathern sling wound round their heads. They took me to the edge of a precipice, and threw down large stones. Presently a she-bear, with two cubs, turned out from a cave below. I shot the old bear dead, and wounded both the young ones, for they stopped a little while by their mother when she first fell, and then made off. We followed up their prints and blood for about a mile, but they both escaped, for a sudden heavy shower of rain prevented our taking their tracks any further. Went back and skinned the old bear; this job the Bheels soon finished, using the large blades or points of their arrows as knives. It was dusk when I regained my tent.

Having, April 6, heard of a large bear who lived in a cave at the top of a very steep hill, just three miles off, I went to seek him. The beast had chased a wood-cutter the day before, but he escaped by climbing a high tree. Taking two men with me to carry my spare guns and the "chagul," or leathern bag to hold water, we walked very silently up the steep hill towards the bear's den, but the brute was wide awake, and bolted out when we were within about thirty yards. A lucky shot rolled him over down the hill side, but he was soon out of sight in the high grass below. From the peculiar moaning noise he made in his descent, we concluded he must be dead, so looked about for a long time, but without again finding him.

After thus losing this bear, I mounted my horse, and rode slowly across country towards my tent, taking with me two Bheels, only one single barrel rifle, and my large dog "Wull" (alias "Vulcan," a queer bred dog, between a Persian greyhound and English bull-bitch, whose name "blackey" had corrupted as above).

We had not gone far when we suddenly met two travellers, who, to our surprise, began to call out loudly, and seemed much frightened. They declared they had just seen a large tiger lying down near the road side, and pointed in the direction he had gone off. Hoping to get a distant shot at the brute, I quickly dismounted, and went after him. On going up to a large thick bush about sixty yards off, to my astonishment out jumped the tiger from the opposite side, and in a few bounds made across the dry bed of a river that was close by. Directly "Wull" saw the tiger, which he doubtless mistook for some new sort of deer, he set off after him, giving tongue all the while, and keeping within two or three yards only of the brute's heels. In vain I whistled and called back the dog, for presently we heard him, evidently baying the tiger among some high reeds and bushes on the opposite bank of the river. Suddenly, one of the Bheels who had followed me called out that the tiger was coming back, and instantly ran off for his life in the surrounding thick jungle. I looked up, and sure enough saw the tiger coming straight towards me, closely followed by the dog.

The beast had nearly recrossed the river bed in a few bounds, and was within thirty yards of me, when, without taking any particular aim, I pitched up the rifle and fired. Then, flinging down the empty gun, I dived among the dense

Lieut W Rice, Delt

TIGER KILLED BY A CHANCE SHOT NEAR "MAIDAH"

thorn bushes, taking in my headlong flight the same road the Bheel had done before me; for while jumping across some wide deep rocks I passed this man, and left him groaning at the bottom of the rocks down which he had fallen, having missed his footing. Being convinced that the wounded tiger was after us, I was uncharitable enough to feel extremely glad that I was not now the last and most likely to be caught by him. The Bheel soon, however, came limping up and rejoined the two travellers in whose charge the horse had been left. While assuring them all that I was certain the tiger was hit, for he threw up his head in the air on my firing, we heard a crashing and panting noise among the bushes; this caused us all to instantly again take to our heels, but the panic was soon over on some one calling out that it was only the dog. After debating some time, the two Bheels agreed to return with me to recover my rifle; and very cautiously we went, half expecting to meet the tiger at every step. At length I found, and quickly reloaded the rifle; and was about to return, when the thought occurred to me to see if there was any blood about the spot where I fired at the tiger. Scarcely had we gone half a dozen paces when, to my great astonishment and delight, I saw the tiger lying quite dead. He had been killed by the merest accident; the bullet, without entering his skull, had grazed the extreme top of it, leaving a long wound, more like a cut from an axe than a ball. This tiger measured eleven feet six inches, and was very stout. With the assistance of some men, who quickly came from a neighbouring village on hearing the news, we carried him to my tent, close at hand.

Strange to tell, my old horse did not show the slightest signs of fear on being taken up to the dead tiger, but coolly smelt him over, though but just killed, and quite warm. The men all agreed that the tiger must have heard my horse's steps, and was no doubt lying in wait for him, but was luckily disturbed by the shouts of the two travellers. The dog

"Wull," by his loud barking, had evidently confused and turned back the tiger on us. For years afterwards, until it was quite worn out, I used his skin as a cover for my bed—sleeping on, instead of inside it, as so easily might have been the case but for such a wonderfully lucky shot.

CHAPTER II.

Signs of the tiger—Peacocks—Monkeys—Crows—Deer—The "Kole balloo"—An unpleasant neighbour—Stumbling on a bear—A fruitless march—Sufferings of wounded bears—The "Korinda bush"—Fate of a wounded tiger.

On the 8th of April we crossed the river "Chumbul," and beat several very likely patches of willow ("jummoneea") cover in the bed of the river, but found no large game. This sort of evergreen tree, for it often attains a good height, forms a cool retreat for tigers during the heat of the day. It grows only where there is plenty of water about, generally in long patches, like small islands in the bed of large rivers, as well as along the banks, and is very thick and shady, much resembling a high-grown osier bed. On beating it, hares, partridges (both grey and painted), and peacocks are started in swarms. The peacock is a most valuable guide to the hunter, from the peculiar note of alarm it invariably utters if there is a tiger or panther moving in the cover. Perhaps, on the noise of the beaters first commencing, a single warning sort of call of "h-a-u-k, h-a-u-k!" (like a note from a trumpet) is heard at intervals from one or more peacocks answering each other from different parts of the cover. At this sound the heart of the sportsman beats high, for he has good cause to shortly expect a sight of his game. If it is followed by the rapid rising of peacocks in succession, each uttering its loud cry of "tok-tok, tok-tok!" as it flies off, evidently in the greatest fright, his hopes amount to a certainty; but sometimes only to be dashed by the appearance at last of some miserable sneaking wild cat, whose approach has been heralded by quite as much calling from the peacocks as if a tiger itself was present. Rarely, and then seemingly only by mistake (for the call is not repeated by the other birds), does a peacock sound the alarm, if merely a bear or any number of hog or deer should be rushing through the bushes crashing down all before them. This is easily accounted for by the fact that they are chiefly preyed upon by the cat tribe. Peacocks, during the heat of the day, are in the habit of hiding themselves under cool shady bushes and rocks, where no doubt they are often pounced upon by wild cats, as well as perhaps by very young tigers, to whom they must afford ample amusement and practice in the art of "stalking" (on perfection in which their future livelihood depends); for no bird is more wary than the peacock. Of course, on quitting his mother's side, having attained size and strength sufficient to knock down an ox or deer, a tiger would disdain such a mere handful of feathers; still, the peacock cannot so easily forget its old enemy; and, therefore, never fails to give timely notice of his presence.

Precisely in the same manner the hunter has a most valuable friend in the common monkey ("hoonumau," *Semnopithecus Entellus*). Troops of them abound in every forest or jungle in the country. In the province of Guzerat they infest the largest cities as well as every village. Being everywhere considered sacred they are never molested, and must consequently lead a very comfortable life, having no enemies to fear but in the woods, where, according to the Bheels' account, panthers and the large rock snake, or boa, are in the habit of preying upon them at night, by climbing the high trees on which the monkeys mostly "roost." This really must be the case, for in the day-time it would be impossible to surprise such watchful animals.

On arriving at a cover which you have decided on beating, frequently a crowd of monkeys are to be seen perched on all the trees around—a pleasant sight, for you are sure to receive from them the most certain information as to the whereabouts of any tiger or panther that may be lurking in the surrounding thickets. Up to this time the tiger is most probably asleep under some shady bush, after the fatigues of the previous evening's foraging expedition. On this point, though, perhaps, aware of his presence, the monkeys are silent enough; but directly he stirs, on the first noise of the beaters arousing him, the monkeys at once commence making a peculiar harsh kind of noise (very different from their ordinary mere chattering, or "hoop, hoop!") which they repeat with great vehemence, as long as and whenever they can obtain even a glimpse of the tiger or panther. This is no doubt intended merely as a warning to their relations to be on the look-out for such a dangerous beast, but it serves equally well to guide the hunter, and tells him plainly what to expect. Like the peacocks, they will not call or "swear" at a bear or other large animals, such as deer or hog. We never knew them deceive us (or "tell lies," as the Bheels remarked) but once, when on silently creeping up, with rifles full cocked, to the spot from whence the noise proceeded, we suddenly came upon a large party of monkeys, who appeared to be merely quarrelling among themselves; for no signs of big game were visible anywhere about. Another good test which the monkey gives of the chance of finding a tiger is this: if on nearing any patch of jungle you may consider worth the trouble of beating, as being likely to hold large game, you should observe any of their number seated on the ground, you may as well pass on, for that cover will contain nothing formidable.

Crows, also, and the common plover or peewit, ("did you do it?") by their incessant calling, will sometimes give notice of a beast, on his quietly attempting to sneak off; but they are not to be depended upon. In the same manner sambur will "bark" or utter a loud kind of bellow, on being disturbed by the sight of either a wild beast or man moving near them. Again the tiger's presence is but too well known by the familiar yell of the "kole balloo," or superannuated jackal; but it is at night mostly that his hideous voice is heard. The "kole balloo" is an aged, mangy, worn-out jackal that has either left or been expelled his pack; being perhaps prevented by his infirmities from any longer being able to get his own living by hunting in company with his fellows, he devotes himself to the service of some tiger. It is his business to discover and give warning of the whereabouts of any stray cattle or animal he may find that will afford his royal master a meal, the remains of which, after the tiger has dined, he of course hopes will fall to his share. Often at night have we been annoyed by his singularly discordant voice (which once heard cannot well be either forgotten or mistaken), well-knowing that a tiger also is close at hand, attracted to our encampment by the old jackal's cry, who has evidently considered our horses, camels, or bullocks, fair food for his master.

On one occasion we distinctly saw a large tiger by the clear moonlight several times pass and repass within a score of paces from where we were sleeping out, in spite even, too, of the large fires kept burning around us, greatly to the terror of our servants, horses, and dog named "Jangeer." The old jackal howled frightfully all the while, close at hand, and no doubt wondered when his meat would be got ready. We did not like to fire at this tiger, for fear, being but slightly wounded, he might charge among us; yet several times in the night he caused us to turn out and show a front. At last, towards dawn, he and the jackal took themselves off, to our great delight.

We crossed the river Chumbul, near "Urneea," on the 9th April, and again looked for sport among the hills. While jumping over some broken rocks, of which these hills seem formed, in rugged masses, piled one above the other, I almost stepped upon a large bear, who was lying asleep between two large pieces of rock. He quickly turned out, evidently but half awake and much confused. I blazed two barrels into him sharp, on which he made off. Unfortunately my spare guns were behind with the beaters, who had, as usual, lagged considerably in the rear; for we were merely going from one likely cover to another at the time. We traced the bear by his blood to a large cave not far off, but could not make him again show himself, although a large heap of dry grass, sticks, and bushes was hastily collected, thrust with long branches into the cave's mouth, and set on fire.

The following day was very wet, heavy and continued showers of rain prevented all thoughts of hunting, so I employed the time in marching towards another range of hills to the north. Did not arrive there till next day, owing to the difficulty of getting the camels up the steep broken track that led over the hills, being obliged to put but a very slight load on them at a time, and make several journeys up and down the hill, before everything could be landed above. I rode quietly on, meeting with but a few "neelghaiee" on the way, at which I did not fire.

Though only a 16 miles' march, my camels did not arrive till the morning of 12th April. I had to sleep out under a tree all night, very hungry, having to wait from breakfast till breakfast time next day. This was an unlucky move, for though I hunted from morning till nightfall for the next six days, I found no large game—the hills being too bare and open. The people of this country would give me no information whatever as to where I should be most likely to meet with sport, nor had I been able before leaving camp to ascertain the best ground to hunt over, so merely wandered from place to place on speculation, judging from the appearance of the country whether it was worth while shooting over or not.

On the 18th April, a Bheel said he knew where a bear was almost certain to be found, so went to the place. It was a deep ravine between two high hills covered with bamboo jungle. Unluckily I was directed to post myself in a bad position, for on being roused by the noise of the beaters, the bear, instead of coming my way, bolted in the very opposite direction. I got only a long shot at him, which, on going to the spot, we found had told, by the marks of blood about, but these we soon lost again, and the ground was too stony to follow up his mere tracks. A bear but slightly wounded does not stop in a hurry, but will make off for miles over the steepest and highest hills at a wonderful pace, leaving the hunter but a very poor chance indeed of again coming up with him. After a race, however, of this kind (whether wounded or not), they must suffer severely, for being unaccustomed to walk about in the heat of the day, which they pass sleeping either in caves or some dense shady cover, turning out to feed only during the night and cool of the morning and evening, their feet get terribly blistered by the hot rocks and stones over which they must run—so much so that on at last killing a bear, after following him up for a long chase, I have often found their feet not only bleeding, but the soles, which are of great thickness, actually partly detached from the flesh.

For the next two days I marched still further north, to try another set of hills round the Fort of "Mandulghur," 16 miles off, but to my disappointment found them very bare indeed, all the brushwood, with which they are covered, having lately been cut down and cleared away; so I hastened across an open well-cultivated plain back towards the hills I had first commenced shooting over.

On the third day, while passing through the small village of "Rajghur," I was told that a tiger lived in a beautiful thick cover of "korinda" bushes, on the borders of a large tank or lake close by. The "korinda" is a very thick evergreen bush, that often attains a great size. It is generally hollow in the centre underneath; the boughs, after rising some few feet, bend over down to the ground, and form a cool shady retreat, much chosen by tigers. The long thin branches are covered with stout sharp thorns, and bear a sweet kind of fruit very like small purple grapes; the blossom, with which the bush at times is quite white, is very sweet, much resembling the orange flower, and can be scented from afar. We never neglected beating any part of the country in which these bushes were plentiful, for they form the most likely of all covers to hold a tiger.

After collecting about twenty men from the village, who seemed eager enough for the sport, I was directed to climb a large tree overlooking a path, down which the tiger would probably pass through the dense high bushes. The men all went round to the other side of the cover, and began making as much noise as possible, beating drums and firing pistols, with which necessary implements of the chase I always travelled. Presently the tiger came bounding by my station; I rolled him over with a ball in his neck, and gave him another in the ribs before he could recover his legs, but he sprang out of sight in the thick surrounding bushes before I could exchange my empty for a loaded gun. There was now the pleasant task in store for me of following up this wounded tiger, so I selected a fine-looking young Bheel to carry my spare gun, and commenced the search. The cover was so dense that we were obliged to crawl on our hands and knees all the time, keeping a very bright look-out, and peering under every bush. This we continued for at least two hours, feeling certain the beast was still lying hid somewhere near at hand, for his prints were nowhere visible on the open plain beyond the cover, but to our surprise without again being able to find the tiger. At last

I was obliged, on its getting dusk, to ride away to overtake my kit that had travelled onwards. A few days after, some one passing that way discovered this tiger by the putrid smell. It had fallen down a deep hole half filled with dead leaves; in our search we must several times have gone close to the place. I unluckily lost this skin, which was a very bright one.

CHAPTER III.

THE "MAN-EATER" OF JAAT—MORE SPORT—HASTY JUDGMENT—VULTURES DISAPPOINTED—ESCAPE AND SUBSEQUENT DEATH OF A TIGER—OLD AND OBSTINATE—RETURN TO CAMP—THE "BAG."

MY leave was now drawing towards a close. On the 22nd April, having descended the hills, my small tent was pitched at the town of "Jaat," a place where a good deal of iron is manufactured, which is dug out of numerous pits in the neighbourhood. After trying a great many likely-looking ravines in the hills all day without finding any large game, I had returned at sunset to my tent, and was dining, when a terrible uproar was heard. A tiger had just carried off a young man close to the town, while driving home his cattle. At once about thirty men armed themselves and rushed after the tiger, making as much noise as they could all the time. After going some little distance they recovered the dead body, which the tiger had dropped, being alarmed, but not before he had eaten the face, hands, and feet off. This poor fellow was seized close to my tent, but at the time I had no idea of what had happened. This tiger had long been known there as a "noted man-eater," and had killed many people lately. It was considered next to impossible to destroy him, for many had watched and tried in vain, because the beast hid all day in the deep unused iron pits, and only came out in the evening to seek prey—but an account will hereafter be given of how it was out-manœuvred and "bagged."

On the 23rd April, I ordered my kit to follow me to the fort of "Gwalior," 9 miles off, while I rode on ahead to look at the country; did not approve of the ground, as the hills were very open and free from bushes, so returned, and stopped the camels at a village called "Dowlutpoora," 6 miles from "Jaat." Here a man told me that he had lately lost several of his bullocks, and thought he could point out where the tiger lived, so we quickly assembled about thirty men, and at once set out for the place. At first sight of the cover my hopes were very great, for it was a beautiful shady ravine, with plenty of water about, besides caves, dense willow bushes, and patches of high green reeds. I was told to lie down on a rock at one end, while all the men in a body silently proceeded to the extremest corner of the cover, and at once began to beat, making a deafening noise. Almost directly a fine tigress made her appearance, and as she attempted to bolt by me was rolled over dead in a few shots, greatly to the delight of the cattle-owners. Skinned her and pegged the skin down close to my tent in the evening.

I set out early on the 24th for "Panghur," six miles off, telling the kit to follow me. At "Panghur," I got together about a dozen men, and proceeded to explore the surrounding country. While passing near the old ruined fort, I heard a tiger roar; and going with the men towards the spot, soon discovered whence the roars proceeded; the tiger being in some thick patches of high grass and bushes scattered around the top of the steep hill. We tried hard to turn out this tiger, in the hope of getting a clear shot at him as he bolted down the open side of the steep hill, but nothing would move this beast, for he merely treated us to more roars as each volley of stones was flung into the thicket by the Bheels, who used their slings for the purpose. So I cautiously crept round and climbed up a tree overlooking the patch of jungle in which we knew the tiger was lying, taking only my light single-barrel rifle with me. Here I soon plainly saw the tiger lying under a thick thorn bush. I fired; my bullet struck him somewhere about the face; whereupon he bolted off with loud roars. After waiting some little time, we, all keeping well together, tried to follow up the blood, but soon lost it. The Bheels, however, knew from the direction he had taken, the ravine into which he would most likely go to hide, so I went ahead, with one man carrying my spare guns, to a point where the tiger would most probably pass, while the rest of the men made a circuit with the view of driving her towards me. Just as we reached the ravine, to my great joy I saw the tiger stretched out at full length, seemingly dead, on a large rock on the opposite bank. On a small tree, immediately overhead, were perched about twenty large vultures, and an "adjutant," while other vultures every moment arrived from all points and settled on the tree. Feeling convinced, from this sight, that the tiger must be dead, I flung up my hunting cap and began to shout for joy, when to the intense astonishment of both the Bheel and self (for he had at once declared his opinion that the tiger was dead), up jumped the beast, and with loud roars made off straight for the point towards which the remaining men were advancing, with the view of driving him towards me. So great was my wonder that I could take but very indifferent aim as she bolted away, and most likely missed both shots. The other Bheels, hearing this noise, at once set up a loud shout, which luckily turned aside the tiger when only about forty yards from them. It was now getting too cool and late to attempt again following up this tiger, so we returned to the fort much astonished at what had occurred.

Here I may as well remark that such an extraordinary fact as the gathering of vultures over a merely wounded tiger never afterwards came under my observation, nor, indeed, over any description of animal so lately wounded as was this tiger.

Next morning I started with the same men at daybreak, taking my two dogs, "Wull" and a greyhound, to assist in finding the wounded tiger. On the way the dogs suddenly pounced upon a small deer, which they surprised sleeping, and killed. While beating along a steep hill side, covered with thick jungle, in which we started several hogs, we presently came upon the tiger; he jumped up and bounded past us roaring loudly. Luckily we were all well together in a body, so he had plenty of room to break back by us, which he did, passing by us within only a few yards; but the cover was so thick that no shot could be had at that time. I quickly got above, and ran on a long way along the top of the hill, in the hopes of overtaking this tiger. Soon a man from below, placed up a high tree to look out, called aloud to say that I had passed the tiger; so after waiting still for about a minute, I presently saw the beast creeping past about twenty yards below me. The first shot luckily killed him dead, passing through his head. We found the marks of yesterday's bullets also on his body. Ordering the body to be carried to my tent to be skinned, I returned there rejoicing to breakfast.

Here, to my further delight, I found the same man who had told me of the tigress killed on the 23rd of April at Dowlutpoora. He reported that another large tiger had taken up his quarters in the very same ravine there, and had already killed two of his bullocks. So I at once mounted my pony, taking only a few biscuits with me for breakfast, and rode round to the different villages near Dowlutpoora, to collect men for the hunt. It was with great difficulty that they would believe me, a tiger having so lately been killed in the same cover.

By this time my guns, which I had ordered to follow me sharp, arrived, and we at once set out for the cover (which is named "Bahara," and has afforded much sport since then). I took up the same position on the rock as before, and soon knew there was a tiger in the cover; for his roars were awful whenever the men approached his hiding-place in a body. After waiting, expecting every moment to see the brute race past me, the men came to say that it was impossible to move this beast, for he still stuck in the same part of the cover in spite of repeated volleys of stones slung there, and innumerable blank discharges from guns. As he declined being driven, I also went to the spot, and was presently assured by a man who had climbed a high tree near, that he could spy a part of the tiger. Quickly slinging my rifle at my back, I was in the act of climbing up the same tree to get a shot, when, all of a sudden, up sprang the tiger, and with extra roars, bounded towards the spot I had just left. So, descending as quick as possible from the tree, I at once ran back outside and above the cover, and was just in time to see the tiger—a perfect monster, and almost free from stripes, old age causing them to appear very faintly marked—slowly passing within about thirty yards below me. I quickly fired five shots, which he acknowledged by more roaring as he sprang into a very dense patch of jungle a few yards further on.

The men all now came up, and much wished to at once proceed to search for this tiger, feeling positive that he must be killed; but of this fact I was by no means so sure. We collected small bundles of grass, which were set on fire and thrown into the cover, a good sized stone being bound up in them to give direction and weight; but the high grass and bushes were too green to burn. The men still urged me to enter the thicket, or let them even go alone, in the bravest manner possible; but this I would not consent to, for fear of an accident happening to some of us. The place was so thick that it would have been impossible to use firearms, nor could we have seen even one yard beyond each step, and might, therefore, have been killed by the enraged wounded tiger, without a chance of defending ourselves.

Hunting ceases to prove sport when it is conducted on mere reckless, foolhardy principles. On it becoming dusk I was reluctantly obliged to leave this tiger, having fourteen miles to go at a foot-pace to overtake my kit, that had been sent on towards camp; for the day before I had received an order to be present in camp to sit on a court-martial, on the 26th of April, 1850. Could I but have remained behind till next morning, no doubt we might have found this tiger either dead or alive; for a whole night makes considerable difference in the powers of any wounded animal; it either gets too stiff to move, or bleeds to death, if at all well "peppered."

Reached my camels and servants by eleven o'clock P.M., awfully tired and hungry. Slept under a tree at Jawud, and rode into camp by daybreak.

My bag, during this trip—alone, and over a country of which I had no previous knowledge, besides being nearly ignorant of the peculiar dialect spoken by the Bheels, one of the greatest drawbacks a sportsman can have—consisted of four tigers killed, and one (this last beauty) wounded; six bears killed and seven wounded—quite sufficient to induce me to start again as soon as leave could be obtained, especially as I considered that a third of my time had been spent uselessly in vain attempts to discover ground fit to hunt over.

CHAPTER IV.

SECOND CAMPAIGN—BEGIN WITH BEAR-MURDER—PHILOSOPHY OF "SPORT"—THE "MAN-EATER" OF JAAT ONCE MORE—MOTHER AND CUB—FACE TO FACE WITH THE FOE—INDIAN GAME PRESERVERS—THEIR MODE OF HUNTING.

IN June I was fortunate enough to obtain, not only leave of absence, but a comrade—Lieutenant Little. He had leave for twenty days, and we proceeded at once to "Jaat," where we arrived on the evening of the 2nd June.

Early next morning, while getting our "battery" in order, a man came to our tent to tell us that a bear had been marked down in a ravine near at hand by some Bheels we had directed overnight to start before daylight and post themselves on the several highest hills around, so as to be able to observe any animal that might be moving about in the cool of the morning; and by watching, give us information as to the precise spot they had chosen to secrete themselves in during the heat of the day. In this manner a bear was seen to enter a thick bamboo cover, and stop there, so he was safely "marked down" until we chose to attend to him—which we at once did—sending the beaters round below to drive him towards us, while we remained ready above the hill to receive him on his making his appearance. The bear was soon started; we allowed him to come close up, and then murdered him.

There, of course, is not half the sport in this way of conducting matters (for killing becomes almost a certainty) that is to be found when you alone have to discover the animal's retreat—when you take up his footprints of the past night, and silently and carefully follow him in all his wanderings up to the joyful and utterly unexpected moment of rousing him from his lair. Then comes the short, sharp, and all exciting encounter, to be followed by a thrill of inexpressible pleasure as you see your late worthy foe quiet on his back, toes uppermost. The result in this latter case is always far more satisfactory and pleasant to recall; still, on stony ground, where "pugging up," or tracking, cannot possibly be carried on, even by the most experienced hunters, or in extremely dense and vast jungles, where hunting for a particular animal is very like the feat of looking for a needle in a bottle of hay, "ringing" any beast, or marking him down, by placing men on the look-out all around his whereabouts, affords about the only possible chance there is of ever meeting with your game; unless, perhaps, you choose rather to resort to the mean trick of watching for him at night, by keeping guard, from a perfectly safe position, over some piece of water that his prints prove he is in the habit of coming to drink at. Still, again, in many places, this often gives the only hope of ever getting a shot at any wild animal, whose skin alone is the desired object, not the sport which his death in a fair fight gives.

The next day, just as we were about to start in search of game, news was brought us that an unfortunate woman had just been carried off by the well-known "Jaat man-eater," while she was cutting grass in company with several other people on a small hill close to the town. This sad account seemed to excite the whole place. A large crowd of men at once volunteered to accompany us in pursuit of this tiger, bringing with them drums, horns, &c., and being, for the most part, well armed, to assist in beating up this brute's quarters. It was very easy work following the course the tiger had taken with his victim, for strips of clothing, hair, and blood, were plentiful enough on the bushes through which he had dragged his prey. Everybody seemed in the highest possible state of excitement, for we momentarily expected to view the tiger as we pressed on—keeping, however, well together—through the high grass and thorn bushes. At length, after following the tracks for nearly two miles, we came upon the body of the poor woman, which the tiger had dropped at the entrance of a long deep cave, or rather the mouth of one of the numerous disused iron pits that were scattered around. She was quite dead, and must have been killed instantly, the back of the skull being smashed in flat.

We now, of course, had greater hopes than ever of putting up the tiger, when, on a sudden, two sambur deer started from out of the long grass in which they had been lying down. Instantly a cry was raised that the tiger was on foot, just ahead of us, so my friend and myself ran forward, in the hope of getting a distant shot, but soon saw the mistake, and returned. The people had now taken up the body, and set off at once for the town, although we much wished them to help in an attempt to smoke out the tiger, who, doubtless, was hid all the while in some cave or pit close by; but this they declined doing, perhaps being only too well aware of the hopelessness of such a job. This tiger was seen by her companions to regularly "stalk" this poor woman; and it was in vain that they shouted in the hope of turning away the beast as he rushed with a roar on his prey.

From "Jaat" we marched to "Rajghur," and beat the same cover of "korinda" bushes in which I had shot a tiger on the 21st April last. Another tiger was quickly started, but he bolted out in a very unexpected direction, so we only got very indistinct snap shots at him. He afterwards rather alarmed our encampment, particularly the horses, for he passed, loudly roaring, within sixty yards of where our tent was pitched, but luckily did no more damage. Next day we again tried the same place, being assured by the villagers that a young tiger had lately been born in the cover; this fact they knew by hearing the little one call at night for its mother. The cover was certainly not above eighty yards from the walls of the village; but tigers become very bold when not molested, and will dwell anywhere, having no fear whatever of men, which is not to be wondered at when they find them ever ready, with the most obliging haste, to give the path on any chance meeting—for who, with no better weapon than a rusty matchlock, or bows and arrows, would like to dispute the point? We threw in a good supply of rockets and "anars," a sort of grenade made of baked clay, and filled with a collection of brimstone, iron filings, gunpowder, &c., which, on being lighted and thrown into a cave, or other place of refuge, is almost sure to make any animal quickly show himself. Unless very carefully made, they are dangerous things to handle, for I once saw a poor old man, who was blowing the touch-paper, to make the "anar" light well, sadly burnt by its unexpectedly exploding in his face, completely singeing off every vestige of beard, eyebrows, and hair, besides temporarily blinding him. These fireworks quickly set fire to the cover, and two tigers were discovered, by their voices, to be in the same small patch of thick bushes. After a great deal of roaring, they both bolted out in opposite directions, but at the same racing pace as did yesterday's tiger. We could only find time to blaze at one of them, and knew our shots had told. Thinking the jungle must now be free from tigers, the Bheels at once entered the thicket; and with much noise, joking, and laughter, began to search for the cub, hoping to take it alive. All this time a troop of monkeys in the trees overhead were loudly "swearing," and seemed much excited. This was considered a sign that they viewed the "kitten," as it tried to dodge its pursuers among the bushes. After waiting some short time, Little and myself agreed to assist in the chase. We left our position and guns behind us, and ran to join in the fun of hunting down the little tiger. While hastening along a narrow path, that led to the spot closely followed by my friend, I saw just at a turn what, at the moment, I fancied could be merely the tail of some village dog, belonging to the beaters, sticking out of a thick "korinda" bush, but to my intense horror, and before I could well stop, found myself face to face with a large tigress, certainly not more than six yards distant; for, on hearing my footsteps, the beast instantly turned round, and looked full at me. Like lightning I dived under a large bush on my right, calling loudly to Little that there was a tiger in the path. At this moment he heard a crashing noise in the bushes close by, which was doubtless caused by the tigress as she rushed past us; though, for the time, he thought it was only some of the numerous peacocks that continued to rise on all sides of us, the cover being full of these birds. I directly ran round to warn the Bheels, still hunting about for the cub, of what had happened. At first they seemed very incredulous, but, on being shown the tiger's prints in the path, they hastily quitted the jungle, and discontinued all further search for the young tiger. Doubtless, this was the tigress that had at first escaped past us unhurt. On hearing the men enter the cover, she must have returned unseen, and was evidently keeping watch. Had the men succeeded in finding her young one, she most certainly would have charged down among them to its rescue. This, they all admitted, would most probably have occurred. It was this tigress, too, at which the monkeys must have so "sworn." We agreed, unanimously, that this little adventure ended happily for all parties concerned in the day's hunting.

On following up the wounded tiger who ran so swiftly by us, he was afterwards found dead, but at least a mile from this place. We next marched to "Kaldahn," a small village four miles off, but had no sport there, although we beat a small likely cover of date-trees, in which a bullock had just been killed by a tiger. The people of this place would afford us no help, for fear of disobeying the "Chief of Begou," who occasionally comes here to hunt. We invariably found that these petty native chiefs were very jealous of our coming to hunt over their districts. In many places they had positively forbidden the people to assist us in any way; an order, it seemed, they dared not disobey, though very willing to have the tigers about their villages destroyed, for their cattle suffered severely from these wild beasts. Several times we were unable, from their opposition, to procure even the commonest supplies (as grass for our horses even), so were compelled to travel elsewhere, although we invariably took good care to pay handsomely wherever we went, well knowing that it was for our own interest to conciliate as much as possible the inhabitants, on whose good will our chances of enjoying sport so much depended.

These insignificant chiefs are occasionally in the habit of themselves turning out with a tremendous retinue to shoot a tiger, of whose whereabouts the most certain information has previously been obtained. Catch one of these lazy gentry ever hunting on speculation, or going any distance for the sport! Their mode of proceedings is as follows:—In the first place several "morchas" or stands, made of stout bows of trees cut down, placed across each other, and then firmly bound together, are "built," at a perfectly ridiculous height for safety sake, up most of the high trees about that command a view of the cover below. Up on these "stands" the chief, with his principal followers, armed with double guns and matchlocks, perch themselves. The whole party is generally very conspicuous, being mostly dressed in white or gaudy-coloured clothes; and because they keep up a continued noise of loud talking, hookah-smoking, &c. At length the beating commences: for this purpose a number of men, pressed most unwillingly into the service, instead of being kept huddled up as closely as possible together, in which formation alone their safety lies, are spread out in a long single line, as if they were about to merely beat up a hare or deer. They thus continue advancing, making their utmost noise, beating drums, blowing horns, firing off matchlocks, with the view of driving the tiger past the positions taken up by the chiefs and their followers in the high trees. The tiger, of course, is soon roused, and, perhaps, at first, allows himself to be quietly driven in the proper direction; but, soon catching sight of his enemies above, naturally halts, and, at once perceiving the trap laid for his destruction, generally turns round, and dashes back with loud roars through the thin line of beaters in his rear, often knocking down one or two unfortunate men who have not time even to get out of his way. Should the tiger, however, prefer to run the gauntlet of the fire from his foes on the platforms in the trees above, often harmless enough, as he bounds off roaring, after rushing past his would-be murderers, he is, of course, pronounced to have been "riddled with balls;" though, to ascertain this last fact, no steps are taken; "following up" the prints or blood of a wounded tiger is a feat utterly unheard of by these mighty princes. Occasionally they do indeed manage to kill the tiger, but rarely does he die unrevenged. From the accounts the natives gave us of all these grand hunting-parties, for at least one man to be killed, or two or three severely "mauled," appeared to be the rule, instead of the exception, at each day's sport. Such "accidents" seem to be so common, that nobody appears the least surprised. These native grandees have a great horror of a blank day, so, to insure sport at short distances from their palaces, the tigers are, in many places, actually preserved, quite as carefully as any game in England, in spite of the havoc they commit on the surrounding country, and no one is allowed to assist in killing them. This we found to be the case particularly towards the Kotah and Boondee country to the north-east of Camp Neemuch, where, but for this prohibition on the part of the native princes, we might have easily made enormous "bags," for tigers literally abound in that beautiful country. There is, perhaps, this excuse to be made: it would be cruel to deprive these chiefs of even one of the few remaining little pleasures left of their former greatness—that is, undisputed right over all animals of the chase in their dominions.

CHAPTER V.

CAUGHT NAPPING — "DISCRETION," ETC. — "NEELGHAIEE" — OUTFLANKED — A LOVELY COVER, BUT NO SPORT—EFFECTS OF A SHOT ON A "DEAD" BEAST—THE "BAG."

THE next day we marched with our kit or baggage as far as the village of "Koree," ten miles distant. While passing through this place, and while the camels and horses made a short halt to drink, Little and myself, each taking merely a double gun with us, set out simply to see if we could find any prints of tigers or other large game about. We persuaded two Bheels and a lad, who were loitering about the village, to accompany us, to point out the most likely ground to look over. Scarcely had we gone even four hundred yards from the village, when, while walking through a small grove of date-trees, I suddenly saw a tigress reclining in the shade of a small palm-tree, certainly not more than a dozen paces from us. Little, at the same moment, caught sight of the beast. It appeared to be dozing during the great heat of the day, and lazily turned round its head to look at us, which gave me time to take good aim, and quickly send a ball through its skull, which was rapidly followed up by two shots in the chest from my friend's gun; these doubled up the tigress in a heap, and it fell dead without even a groan. Directly the men with us caught a glimpse of what we were firing at, with the most laughable haste they sprang into the first trees at hand, from which we could not persuade them to descend even after we had pulled out the tigress from under the bush by its tail and hind legs, so astonished did they seem at the whole proceeding. At length they came down and helped us, with some other men quickly called from the village, to carry the tigress to our tent, which we ordered to be pitched in a place where we had so soon met with game. These men did nothing but stare, and seemed almost speechless with wonder. Altogether it really was a very lucky finish for us, being so slightly armed, no spare guns being at hand, in case our first shots had not taken such good effect.

That same evening, while one of our grooms was taking a horse down to drink at a stream near the village, he saw a large tiger, and quickly ran back to give the news. We ran out after him at once, taking all our guns with us, but he was not then to be seen; so we commenced looking about for him in some patches of high grass hard by. At last, leaving our servants with the spare guns on one side, we were in the act of crossing a small stream, when the tiger got up out of some long grass in the bed of the river about forty yards before us, and quietly trotted off into the surrounding jungle. Having only one gun each with us at the time, we were afraid to fire, lest he should charge us or our men on the low bank, for they were standing together in the tiger's direction. This tiger was a very large one indeed: though sorry enough to so lose him, still we felt we had only acted prudently, and trusted to again meeting him when better prepared.

We moved our tent next morning three miles, to the village of "Chuldoo," and had scarcely arrived there when a cowherd came running to tell us that he had just seen a tiger enter a grove of date-trees close to the walls of the village. We at once got together about a dozen men, and started for the spot. After quietly looking about for some time, we spied a part of the tiger's skin, but could not tell whether his head or tail was towards us; he was lying in the shade of a clump of low date-trees. Silently as possible, after placing our spare guns on the ground in front of us, having previously sent all the men to the rear, so as to be out of danger, with the exception of one, who was directed to climb a high date-tree near at hand, and look out, we knelt down within twelve yards of the enemy, and prepared to fire a volley by word of command. Unfortunately one of the guns, being damp, would not go off, but the tiger did, for he instantly sprang up with loud roars, and, most fortunately for us, bolted off, crashing through the bushes in exactly the opposite direction. Having called the men, we now all together commenced following up the blood, of which there was plenty, and soon came upon the tigress dead in some high grass not very far from where we had fired on it.

In the evening a herd of "neelghaiee" (a species of wild half-deer half-cattle sort of animal) came down to drink at a stream near our tent; we gave them a volley in the hope of supplying our followers with meat, but did not bag one. These harmless animals will carry off any amount of lead, unless struck on the head or other vital part. The flesh is coarse and tasteless, with the exception of the hump of the male or "blue bull" and the tongues. Their marrow-bones, moreover, are not to be despised. The does or cows are of a fawn colour, but the old bull is of a dark slate colour, and stands at least six feet high, or rather more. The natives covet parts of his hide, which is very thick, to make their shields of. In many places they are very common and tame, and so afford no sport to shoot, but in the plains they have the art of getting over the ground at a long easy swing canter which puzzles even a good horse to close with them; so they are sometimes hunted with the spear, giving famous long runs.

From "Chuldoo" we marched to "Ambah," five miles. Here we heard that a tiger had lately been killing a number of bullocks, so several men at once offered to point out his usual haunt. After beating a very thick and likely cover, which, however, proved blank, we were returning home, for it was too late in the day to continue hunting, when suddenly the tiger got up out of some long grass in the bed of a river along which we were walking. Only a mere glimpse could be obtained of him, so we could not then fire; but as he seemed inclined to make for the cover we had just finished beating, we, taking two Bheels with us to carry our spare guns, at once ran back in the hope of meeting this tiger on his entering the cover. Very nicely too we managed it, and had just taken up our position on a low rock, when we were startled by a loud roar immediately behind us; we turned round and fired a volley in what seemed the right direction (for it was rather too dark to clearly distinguish anything in the high grass), which was followed by fresh roars; our two men all the time behaving admirably, quickly handing us the spare guns, without even dreaming of bolting, though this tiger was very close indeed to us, and the row he made was truly awful, being so unexpected. It seems he must have made a circuit to gain this cover, and so come upon us unawares, and merely roared to show his annoyance at our presence there. We agreed to have another look for him next morning; so thinking we knew now his usual hiding place, we went alone very silently on tip-toe to the cover, but by ill luck mistook the exact spot by only about a dozen yards, and had the mortification of seeing him get up and walk off into very dense jungle without the chance even of firing a shot, his feet and tail only being visible, whereas we did hope to catch him napping and blow his brains out; as it was, we were within thirty paces, but could not fire, owing to the thick bushes.

From "Ambah" we moved on to "Limree," six miles, having a terrible steep hill to descend. The road was a mere track, in many places blocked almost up by large masses of rock that had rolled from the hills above. This was very awkward work for the poor camels, as they were accustomed only to smooth, level roads; we were obliged to unload them and make several trips up and down for the extra baggage. At this place we discovered a most beautiful ravine, named "Kokee."

In fact, I do not know a more likely spot to find large game in. It is a cover about two miles long, full of high green reeds, "jummoneea" bushes, or patches of a kind of willow-tree, with a stream running through the whole length. The sides are perpendicular walls of red rock, full of caves. There are also clumps of bamboo jungle in parts, and the whole place looks very wild and picturesque. Unluckily, some chiefs had hunted here the day before we came, putting out a tiger, which as usual escaped them. Nevertheless, we beat through the whole cover, but without finding any large game, which did not cause us much surprise, knowing how lately it had been disturbed.

Our next marches were along the hills where in my last trip I had found so many bears; but though we moved by easy stages, and most carefully hunted over every inch of the ground, strange to tell, we did not succeed in finding another bear. Sambur, as usual, were plentiful, but, expecting nobler sport, they were let off.

Arriving at the village of "Deypoora," three miles from "Ruttenghur" fort, we were here told of a tiger that had lately killed very many bullocks, so started with several men to look him up. We were taken to a ravine in the plains named "Loonee," and had taken up our position on a rocky ledge, when we were recalled by a man who had seen the tiger. He directing us to the spot, we cautiously advanced, and looking over the steep bank of the ravine, saw the tiger stretched out at full length, just three yards or less below us. He looked up and grinned horribly; we instantly gave him a bullet each, whereupon he sprang into the cover below, and was out of sight even before we could get a second shot. On going down the bank we soon found drops of blood, and easily carried these on for some distance down the ravine, when all at once they entirely ceased. The ground was bare sheet rock, or large slabs of flat stones, so no foot-prints could be discovered. After going on some little distance, we met a man tending a herd of goats, who denied having seen the tiger pass, and indeed it was but too evident, from the unconcerned manner in which the goats browzed and cropped the bushes around, that they had seen no such formidable animal lately. So we retraced our steps to again search for the blood, when suddenly a man by signs pointed to a cave formed by a large ledge of rock that had fallen from above. We knew his meaning, though it much surprised us, for we had only just passed close by this very place, looking for the tiger's prints. All the men, as usual, were at once ordered to a safe distance in the rear, while, placing our spare guns before us, we knelt down to polish off this tiger at an unpleasantly close distance; for we were prevented by a steep bank behind us from going farther back, and a view could not be obtained from any other point. As it was, all we could make out were the tiger's *two eyes* shining very clearly in the dark cave with an indistinct outline of his face. We silently agreed to fire together on the word "one," "two," "three," being given by one of us. On the smoke clearing away, we were delighted to see our foe stretched out stiff on his back, the white of his belly being uppermost and very visible. On going nearer, two small holes, one over each eyebrow, from which streams of blood flowed, caused us to congratulate each other on our good aim. We now walked close up and saw that the cave in which this tiger had tried to hide himself, although it had but a small entrance, was large enough inside.

While talking over our lucky shots we observed one of the tiger's arms slowly move, but as if from mere muscular action, caused by its weight and the position the beast was lying in. On noticing this, I suggested that another shot should be given to make sure, but Little slightly objected, on the ground that it was only uselessly making holes and so spoiling the skin. On this I agreed to fire where our knives would first be used in taking off the victim's jacket, so at once, while we were looking into the cave, without putting my gun to my shoulder, I placed its muzzle opposite the tiger's chest and fired the remaining loaded barrel. All this time the men, who from a distance had seen us so near the tiger's den, came running up towards us in a great state of delight at their enemy being killed; for so they and we both thought was indeed the case. Instead of which, no sooner had I fired than, with a frightful roar, up jumped the tiger, as lively as ever. With one bound, Little, who is remarkably strong and active, gained the top of the high ledge of rock that formed the tiger's cave. Here he kept guard with his spare loaded barrel pointed over the mouth of the den; our other guns we had left on the ground on walking up to first look at the tiger. For my part, in the most dreadful state of alarm, I at once rushed through the men who had now come up and were crowding round us, upsetting three or four and myself in so doing. For the moment there was a terrible panic, and the ground being very uneven and stony, everybody seemed to fall over and trip up everybody else. Some climbed small trees like monkeys; while others in their fright ran clean out of sight without stopping to look behind. All this time the tiger was roaring awfully. I fully believed that he was outside the cave, killing each man as he caught them, instead of which, being much confused, he luckily remained in the den, round and round which he kept walking, seemingly without being able to find his way out. At last, on gaining my legs, I snatched up a gun and climbed up a small thin tree, just in front of the den. There were two men already in this slight tree, so its branches bent down unpleasantly close to the ground with our weight. From this point I fired twelve more shots, at only as many yards' distance, into this tiger before he was quiet; only his fore arm and lower part of his belly could be hit every time he appeared at the mouth of the cave. All now being still, we came down from our high posts, and this time found the beast really dead, riddled with balls. The appearance of the ground was very laughable; guns, drums, bows, spears, shoes, turbans, were scattered all over the place. Some poor fellows were sadly bruised. It appeared that our shots had merely for the time stunned this tiger, missing his brain, which lies in a long narrow cell directly between the eyes and on the extreme top of the forehead. The shot in his chest most effectually revived him.

This was a most extraordinary and lucky escape for all of us, for, supposing him quite dead, we should have begun to haul him out of the cave, and at once proceeded to skin him on the spot; during which operation, the beaters usually all crowd round and discuss the brute's death, and recall the losses he has occasioned in his day. Taking off his skin would, no doubt, have revived the tiger, when the consequences that might have ensued are terrible to conceive; doubtless more than one life would have been lost. This little adventure served as a good caution to us never to fear making holes in a beast's skin to fully ascertain whether he was dead or not. At this time we were but young hands at tiger-killing, but have since learnt, by experience, many such valuable lessons. This tiger was a very large old one.

We continued to hunt along the hills by easy stages as far as "Doraee" village, but found no more sport. Our leave of absence having now expired, we had to ride back to camp twenty-eight miles, which we reached just in time; for the "monsoon," or rainy season, commenced immediately afterwards.

Altogether, we were satisfied with the sport obtained in this trip. Our bag consisted of four tigers killed and one wounded, also a bear killed. Another sporting expedition was determined on for the next "hot season," and great were the preparations of drums, fireworks, ammunition, knives, pegs, and arsenical soap for skinning and preserving the skins of the animals slain.

We also borrowed every gun that was to be lent, and raised the "sinews of war;" for tiger-hunting in Rajpootana is not so lucrative an employment as in many other parts of India. The Government reward for each skin is only ten rupees, or one pound sterling; for a panther, five rupees, or ten shillings, with nothing for bears.

CHAPTER VI.

THIRD CAMPAIGN—GAME SOON FOUND—THE HUNTER'S DRESS AND TACTICS—LOSE THE GAME—EFFECTS OF DISOBEDIENCE—HUNTING THREE TIGERS—CHARMS—TIGER TACTICS—THE "MAN-EATER" OF JAAT KILLED AT LAST—THE TRIUMPH THEREUPON—DEATH OF ANOTHER OLD ACQUAINTANCE—A GALLANT PANTHER SHOT FLYING.

WE commenced our third expedition in March, 1851, having obtained leave of absence from the 14th day of that month to the 14th June, 1851, for the express purpose of shooting large game. Having sent on our small tent and servants to "Panghur," twenty miles north of Camp Neemuch, we rode out there on the evening of 14th March. We had not long to wait for action. Early next morning news was brought to us of a tiger having been seen close at hand by some men we had sent out before daylight to look out on the surrounding hills.

It was some time before we were ready to start, having to arrange our "battery," and separate the ammunition for our respective guns and rifles, which were of many different bores. This is often a serious nuisance to the hunter, who, in the haste of quickly reloading, is obliged to be very careful not to ram the wrong bullets down the wrong gun. However, we got away by nine o'clock A.M., and, having stationed ourselves at the side of a ravine, in which the game was said to be lying, sent the beaters round to the other end of the cover, first placing a man up a tree to keep guard over a likely place by which the tiger might possibly attempt to leave the cover before passing our position. It was this man's duty on observing the tiger attempt to approach the path over which he was so safely placed, to "head" back the game, which is easily effected, either by a slight cough, or tapping two stones together. In fact any slight unusual noise will instantly cause a tiger to retire as he comes slowly creeping along, keeping the brightest possible look-out for the least suspicious looking object in his path ahead, for his sole desire on being roused by the beaters is to make his escape unseen, well knowing that so unusual and great a noise in his otherwise seldom disturbed retreats bodes him no good. For this purpose, to as much as possible avoid being observed, we took good care to have our dress of a brown colour, so as to make it very difficult, even at a very short distance, to distinguish us from the rocks and jungle around. At this hot time of the year, all vegetation being dried up, the country presents, for the most part, a general brown tint, but, of course, of many different shades. Owing to this precaution, as well as by invariably preserving the strictest silence, and by remaining perfectly still, we were very rarely indeed detected in the positions we had chosen, or where we attempted to hide ourselves, by any wild beasts we hoped to kill, though they frequently approached us extremely close before we deemed it time to let them know of our vicinity. This regard to one's dress is absolutely necessary; for tigers, and nearly all large wild animals, are extremely cautious, espe-pecially if they have been shot at before; when they would, to a certainty, prefer the risk of breaking back past the beaters, in spite of the dreadful din they were making, to facing any strange object they may have discerned, but cannot clearly make out, in their path ahead. This was our sole reason for always directing the beaters to keep well together. Better let any amount of game escape back than have one accident from the men straggling about singly when there are so many chances of the tiger meeting and knocking over, in his flight, individuals whom he would carefully have avoided, provided they kept in a compact body, and allowed him room to pass. To prevent this risk as much as possible, we made it a rule never to fire until he had quite passed our position, when the beast, if not killed, was sure to bolt forward.

In this instance, the beating having commenced, we soon received notice of the tiger having broken cover by his voice as he passed immediately in rear and above the bank on which we were lying hid. We could not see him, but well knew he was much enraged by the continued growls he kept up as he passed. He finds it, of course, very provoking to be suddenly awoke from sleep, and to have to run barefoot for perhaps a mile over rocks and stones almost red hot; for the tiger, from only seeking its prey at night, or in the cool of the day, feels the excessive heat severely, and often refuses to leave his stronghold in spite of all the hunter's means—fireworks, guns, stones, noise—if there is no other retreat near, and he has to attempt his escape across an open, burning, rocky plain. The fact was, the man in the tree had failed to keep a good look-out, and so allowed the tiger to creep past his post unobserved. This we afterwards discovered to be the case by retracing the animal's prints, wishing to find out how we had been outmanœuvred so easily by the tiger. We followed up the prints, and twice again started the tiger. This we knew to be the case by his loud roars close in front of us; but we could neither get a shot, on account of the thick jungle.

Returned to our tent, vexed at losing this tiger, by evening. Hunted next day in another direction, but without success; returning homewards, we again put up yesterday's tiger in the same cover, but could not see him, only heard his voice. Moved our tent to "Dowlutpoora," six miles, and set out early to beat the "Bahara" ravine there, fresh prints of a tiger having been found in that beautiful cover. Soon, a fine tiger bounded out for a few yards, but quickly returned to the dense thicket. Being too far off, we did not then attempt to fire at him, in the hope that he would come nearer the rocky ledge on which we were posted. Our men tried hard to dislodge this tiger, but were unable to do so; nor would the cover burn, being too green to take fire. At length a Bheel, named "Chutra" (the same man that last year told me of two tigers in this very place), being angry at having his bullocks killed lately by these beasts, vowed he would turn out this tiger, so left the rest of the beaters, who, according to our strict orders, had remained on the outside of the cover, and rushed down into the dense bushes sword in hand. The poor fellow was almost immediately seized by the tiger, and mauled severely, being much bitten about the shoulder and arms, and clawed on the legs. On hearing this happen, the other men in a body rushed to the rescue at once, drove off the tiger, and brought the wounded man outside with them.

All this time we had no idea of what had occurred, being at some distance watching for the tiger's appearance. We hastened to the spot on hearing of the accident, and, having sent some of the men to carry home the wounded Bheel to his hut, tried hard to persuade the rest to accompany us into the cover, but they refused, although a body of men could easily have forced their way through the dense bushes, yet for two only to have attempted doing so would have been mere rashness. So we were obliged to let this tiger alone for a time. We next went to see how the Bheel was getting on, and left a good sum for his maintenance with his relations, who promised to take every care of him. He was quite sensible, but much shaken. The other men tried at the time to dissuade him from entering the cover, but he would not listen to their advice. This was the first accident any of our men had met with while hunting with us, but it could not be helped, for the man wilfully disregarded all orders.

We now rode on twelve miles to "Rajghur," where the kit had been sent. For the next two days no game could be found in this neighbourhood, or prints even, except those of a panther; but this brute was nowhere visible. On the third morning a Bheel brought us news that three tigers had been lately seen in a patch of jungle, about two miles distant; so off we started for the place with about thirty men. The cover being very wide we took up separate positions, from which we could overlook the best part of it, which consisted of clusters of thick thorn bushes scattered about in some high grass on level stony ground. .At first, rather to our surprise, it was drawn blank. Five of the beaters now positively declared that they had caught a glimpse of the three tigers, but this fact the others seemed to doubt, so we went to look for prints on the spot they pointed out; but could see none, the ground being too rocky. While we were discussing what was next to be done, a most unmistakeable roar was heard about thirty yards from where we were all standing together. On quickly sending a man up a tree close by to look out, he saw several men running off in the opposite direction. Presently we were joined by a woodcutter, who seemed in a great state of alarm; he said that while walking a little before his companions, who had come to cut down trees in this jungle, he met a tiger, and only escaped by throwing himself flat on his face as it rushed by him.

We hereupon hastened to our old positions, while the men went round to again beat the cover. Soon two large tigers and one half grown passed by my post, but as I could not get a clear shot, on account of the dense brushwood, I allowed them to pass on to Little's position without firing. I soon after heard him fire two shots. It appeared he had only seen one tiger come by alone, which quickly bounded out of sight in the high grass, on his firing, before he could get another shot at her. The other tigers must have turned away from his position, for he saw but one go by. Having so lately had a man wounded, and the jungle being so dense, we used extra precautions in following up this tiger; so observing the way the slight wind was blowing, we set fire to the grass, and advanced in a body behind it, in the hope of either getting more shots if the tiger started before us, or, if dead, of being able to save the skin before the flames should reach it; but in this last hope we were deceived, for after going about a few hundred yards, which took half an hour's time, we came upon the dead tiger, over which the fire had just passed, singeing off its hair, and so spoiling completely the skin. The smoke from the burning grass had prevented our seeing the body in time to save the skin. We cut off the beast's head and claws, besides taking out the "collar bones."

These are two small bones about four inches long, bent like a bow; embedded in a mass of muscle in the tiger's fore-arm, they are quite disconnected from any other bone, and are only to be found in the panther, tiger, or lion. The natives superstitiously regard them as "charms" against evil, and have the same notion of the tiger's claws, a pair of which are worn by their children round the neck for protection against all harm. The Bheels call these bones "goojbul," and say their use is to give more force to the tiger's blow, when with his paw he strikes down his prey.

To-day, while looking for this wounded tiger, we found a most curious land tortoise, beautifully variegated, of a description that neither we nor any of the Bheels had ever before seen; so it must be of a very rare species indeed, for their whole lives being spent in the woods, they must have observed others, if at all of a common sort.

The next day we hunted over three large covers about a mile apart for the remaining two tigers, but could nowhere find them, although we saw their fresh prints. The rocky nature of the ground prevented their being "pugged up."

At night we were kept awake by the continued roaring of a tiger near our encampment. It is rather singular that tigers should indulge in making this seemingly unnecessary noise at night, for any one would imagine that such a row was enough to scare every sort of deer, on which they chiefly subsist, out of the country. The Bheels thus account for such extraordinary conduct, which version I firmly believe to be correct. Tigers for the most part confine themselves to one particular district of perhaps a few square miles in extent, with every inch of which ground they are of course thoroughly acquainted. As night draws on, the tiger will be heard to roar at several different points, separated at a good distance from each other; this is done with the view of disturbing the deer that might be lying in the neighbourhood, and driving them for safety to some more distant part of the jungle, to which the tiger next, silently enough, betakes himself. The deer being thus congregated in one quarter, for they also frequent only particular districts, the tiger, by either lying in ambush over some piece of water at which they will most likely soon come down to drink, or by sallying forth among them, has of course a double chance of securing some victim, with not half the trouble of hunting him up over a large tract of country. This seems far more likely to be the case than that, as some suppose, Providence has purposely caused the tiger to give this timely warning of his presence to the deer and smaller animals to enable them to make their escape, which otherwise would be in a fair way of being speedily exterminated by such a cunning, silent, savage enemy.

From "Rajghur" we marched to "Jaat," beating a ravine on the road, near which we heard a bullock had yesterday been killed, but did not find any game worth firing at. The men started a bear, but we did not see it. On arriving at "Jaat," we collected as many men as possible over night, intending to have another try for our old enemy the "man-eater" here, still the terror of the neighbourhood. Our plan was by starting at the first break of day to see if we could not cut off the tigress

Lieut. W. Rice Delt.　　M. & N. Hanhart lith.

before it returned from its night foraging wanderings over the adjacent plain to lie up for the remainder of the day in its stronghold among the disused iron pits. The idea and chase seemed highly popular, for many men at once agreed to accompany us; so we betook ourselves to the iron pits, and then directed the men to spread themselves out over a large extent of ground and commence beating towards our position from a long distance. At this cool time of the morning there was no danger in thus separating the beaters, for we knew the tigress, if out in the plain at all, would at once make direct for its den on hearing the slightest noise. Our calculations were well founded, for scarcely had we heard the first faint noise of the drums and pistol-shots, when to our inconceivable joy we saw from a long way off the tigress making direct for our post. We allowed her to come at a long trot close on within about ten yards, when both our rifles simultaneously discharged dropped her. Two other shots made the kill secure. Great was tho excitement of the people on hearing of our good luck, men at once ran off with the news, and the whole populace turned out to meet us on our return with the body, which was carried in triumph on small trees, hastily cut down for the purpose, through the town to our tent. Here we were met, as in this part of the country seems usual, by a bevy of females, the youngest and fairest of whom advanced and presented us with bunches of gay flowers, while the rest continued loudly singing some poetry in praise of all tiger-killers, generally recited on these occasions. Altogether a very pretty custom, quite dramatic! We got back to our tent about an hour after sunrise.

Before proceeding to skin this tigress, the people much wished us to await the arrival of a Bheel from some distance, whom they had sent for. It appeared that some time ago this man was cutting grass, in company with his brother, near this town, when the tigress suddenly sprang out upon his brother and carried him off, but not before the poor fellow had given the brute a severe cut with his small sickle over the face. All this was distinctly seen by the surviving brother, who, on his arrival, at once pointed out a deep scar or seam, now healed up, across the tiger's forehead. This at once removed all doubt as to this very brute being the noted "man-eater," which was afterwards confirmed by the fact that on our again visiting this place for three successive years, we heard of no other person being killed in the interim; although the people assured us that it had murdered in the preceding two years upwards of forty persons of this town alone. Thus ended the reign of terror so long established and well enforced of this rapacious pest. Appearances proved that she had left a hopeful family dependent on her well-known system of foraging. The evening before her death she had killed two bullocks, besides lying in wait for, and much terrifying a horseman, who was travelling towards "Jaat." This man narrowly escaped the beauty and her two young ones that accompanied her. It was from hearing his account of her being out in the plain that we planned the successful manœuvre which ended in the death of this tigress. She measured ten feet and a few inches; her tusks were, from some cause or accident, quite worn down, although she seemed in full vigour and very fat. Crowds of people from all the neighbouring villages came to look at it during the day; so we held quite a "levee." All agreed that no other method would probably have succeeded in destroying this cunning plague, for she had baffled many attempts.

We now determined to make another attempt to kill the tiger that wounded our beater on 18th March; and knowing the hopelessness of expecting any of the "Dowlutpoora" men to assist us after the accident that had happened to their fellow villager, we started with forty-seven Bheels of this place to storm the cover where we were told this tiger still held possession. We reached the place, six miles off, by 9 A.M.; and having agreed to beat the ravine in a different direction, took up our position.

It was by no means an enviable one, for we were on a bank or ledge of rock not four feet high, which was commanded from above, had the tiger appeared in our rear, and was merely sloping, in parts nearly level, below. However there was no better hiding place about. Almost directly the beating commenced, our enemy appeared most unexpectedly close. We instantly greeted her with the contents of our double rifles, which rolled her over, while another volley quite settled the business. This was a fine tigress, with a beautiful bright skin. Having thus had our revenge, we next went to see how the wounded Bheel was getting on, but finding him still in a bad way, he was at once started on a cot, carried by four men, for Camp, in charge of one of our servants, to have the benefit of the scientific attainments of our talented friend Dr. M——e, 25th N.I. This man soon recovered, and often afterwards pluckily assisted us to kill other tigers.

We rode back to "Jaat" in the evening. On the 26th March, while looking about, the fresh prints of a large tiger were discovered leading into a deep ravine. We mustered all our men, and started to beat the place. We had taken up our position on a very steep bank, and were anxiously waiting for the tiger's appearance, when, just as the noise of the beaters commenced, we were surprised by a stone falling from above and a little to the right of where we were posted. On looking up, we saw a splendid panther coming straight towards us. This compelled us to fire; had he been merely passing, as we were after nobler game, we should have let him alone for the time. We struck him with four bullets, on which he bounded down a small branch of the big ravine and was lost to sight, but only for a few moments; for, thinking he was bolting off, we each seized a spare gun and were running after him to get a parting shot, when, to my astonishment, I saw the panther in the act of charging down from a high rock directly over head. Instantly stopping short, I blazed both barrels into the beast, and then sprang off the rocky ledge on which we were standing into a small tree below.

Little, seeing me fire, immediately got ready, and as the panther was in the act of leaping after me, by an admirable shot in the head, actually rolled him over in the air while making his spring in a most determined charge. The panther came tumbling down head over heels, completely doubled up, through the boughs of the tree into which I had jumped, and fell dead at the foot of it. Little was only about three or four yards off at the time he made this wonderfully lucky shot, which no doubt saved me from a good "mauling, is not even worse.

We silently and quickly reloaded the empty guns, making signs to the men who came running up on hearing our shots, in the full conviction that we had killed the large tiger, to go back and continue the beating by rolling down the steep sides of the ravine large stones and rocks, which they directly recommenced doing, for we much feared that the tiger, having heard our shots in his front, would break either back or sideways out of the cover, instead of coming on, which, however, he fortunately did, for in a few minutes afterwards we saw a splendid fellow bounding up the steep sides of the ravine immediately opposite our first position, to which we had now returned. In another moment or so he was roaring and biting at everything near him, having received four rifle-balls in his body, one of which luckily broke his back. The rest of our "battery" soon finished him. The distance was at least ninety yards where he fell. Without double flush-sighted rifles we could not have made such good practice at the pace he was going. This was the finest tiger we had as yet killed; he measured eleven feet eleven inches, counting from the end of his nose, between the ears, to the tip of his tail, and his head was enormous. Both the beasts, after they had been disembowelled to reduce the weight, were carried on tree-stumps with a good deal of trouble, the

JAAT PANTHER CHARGING.

ground being very stony and broken, to our tent, where we skinned and pegged them down, afterwards rubbing in the arsenical soap to preserve the skins, before sunset. Altogether our good day's sport seemed to rather astonish the natives of these parts.

CHAPTER VII.

OUR MEN FAIL IN THEIR DUTY—"SAMBUR," THEIR USES—OTHER DEER—"WILD DOGS"—FIRE AND KILL—FORMATION WHEN "FOLLOWING UP"—EFFECT ON THE TIGER—A CHARGE, ITS LAUGHABLE RESULTS—YOUNG BEARS—"TWO IN A BUSH"—CRY OF "A MAN KILLED!"—ONLY "MAULED."

CONTINUING our operations, we set out on the 27th March to beat a ravine called "Amko;" the men put out a bear, but we did not then see him. They pointed out the direction in which he had gone, and presently we saw him quietly climbing up a distant hill. Off we ran at our best speed, and luckily came upon him, lying up in some bamboo clumps or bushes. We instantly gave him three shots, which, luckily, finished his existence, fortunately without any charging taking place, for we had no spare guns up with us at the time, having left the men far behind in our race after the bear.

In many instances, when running after big animals in the hope of overtaking them, or of getting a parting shot as they made off, we used to find that we had far outstripped the men who carried our spare guns, and who were required, at least, to be able to keep up in a chase of this sort. This did not arise from our being able to compete with these men in the art of getting over broken ground, but solely from the fact that the gun-carriers had not the same interest in the chase. As it was quite a matter of indifference to them whether we killed or not, they took matters more easy, and lagged behind. This lazy conduct often left us an ugly chance of being overmatched on attacking the beast we had overtaken: a strong argument in favour of a repeating rifle.

Afterwards we looked for game in some other good covers about, but without success. Returning to our tent, I smashed the fore leg of a fine buck sambur, with splendid horns, but he managed to get off, for it was a shot at least 200 yards, as the noble looking animal stood watching us from a distant rocky peak. It was rather late in the season for him to wear his horns, for they generally shed them at the beginning of the hot weather. Provided we felt certain that there was little chance of getting a shot at any wild beast in the neighbourhood, we seldom neglected killing sambur, solely for the sake of their skins. The leather is beautifully soft and thick. From it we had shoes and gaiters made, which never, by any chance, hurt the feet, though ever so new or ill made. The skin easily stretches, being very pliable, and so smooth that it was quite unnecessary to wear socks with these boots. This leather, moreover, is the very best possible protection from thorns, and seldom ever tears. It makes also capital covers for saddles, which otherwise would soon be worn out and spoilt in such rough work as "hog hunting," or knocking about for months in the jungles. The flesh is coarse in the extreme, and very tasteless, but the marrow-bones are excellent.

On one occasion, I well remember, we were glad enough to live on sambur meat for more than a week, being out of supplies, and far away in the woods from where any better food could be procured. If sambur are started from any place, it argues but little chance of your finding either tiger or panther in that particular cover; but instances did occur in which this rule was upset, so we mostly allowed the sambur to escape, lest, by firing at them, a shot might be lost at more worthy game; otherwise, almost any number could have been slaughtered, as they dashed past us at only a few yards' distance, often in herds of even twenty together, in particular places where at all numerous. Where sambur abound, there will surely tigers be also found, but not living in the same patch of jungle or cover.

The Bheels with us were always very desirous that we should shoot these animals, as well as the "cheetul" or spotted deer ("axis"), for them to eat. They also contrive to kill them even with arrows, silently following for miles on the wounded deer's tracks. They have even a better chance of "bagging" the sambur with an arrow than with the small bullet used with their matchlocks, for the long broad blade of the arrow, the points or heads of which serve them for all the purposes of a knife, by cutting deep at each stride of the poor wounded deer, soon causes him to stop and seek for safety, by endeavouring to hide itself in some dense cover, where, however, it is soon spied by such lynx-eyed gentry as the Bheels. It is perfectly astonishing how close deer will sometimes lie when thus hiding themselves. I have even fired into them quite near, but without their showing the slightest sign of having been struck, when, on attempting to lay hands on them, they will start off again seemingly none the worse.

The "cheetul" are very handsome creatures (about the same size as fallow deer, and spotted in the same manner), and are in some jungles, where there is plenty of water and shade, very numerous—it being no uncommon sight to meet them in herds of even a hundred or more together; but the meat, like that of the sambur, is nearly as coarse and rank. Besides these deer, we often disturbed the little "beadlah," or "beekree," a small sort of four-horned deer, that somehow appears to have a touch of the sheep in his make. These deer are found singly, or at most in pairs; they lie during the heat of the day in thick high grass, or cool shady ravines, and start up even at the hunter's feet, bounding off in a series of quick high jumps, rendering it difficult to shoot them with ball, though so close. At evening they are often heard calling—a queer bleating sort of bellowing noise. The flesh is first-rate, far superior to any other kind of deer, and very tender. So, on returning from our day's sport to the tent, we generally looked out for a shot at these little creatures for the pot. The fact of their meat being so good, may be perhaps accounted for from their never exposing themselves to the sun. The tiny "mouse," or little hog deer (for they have tusks like a boar, but on a very small scale), we did not meet with in this part of the country, neither did we see many jungle fowl, so common in most large forests, but the little spur fowl, less even than the smallest bantam, were numerous enough.

Wild dogs, too, seemed to be utterly unknown in this country, which seemed rather strange considering their numbers in other wild extensive jungles over which we had hunted, where they were often met with in packs of even thirty or more together. The wild dog is about eighteen inches high, of a brick red or bright fox colour, with a thick bushy tail tipped with black, the ears are also black, pointed, and upright. They are the most determined enemies of the tiger, hunting him whenever they meet with him. I have been assured by Bheels that they have sometimes seen a tiger kept prisoner up a large tree with a pack of these dogs baying around him, when on no other occasion would a tiger attempt to save himself by climbing trees. On the approach of the men the wild dogs dispersed, when the tiger jumped down, and gladly made his escape. This I firmly believe to be a fact, for the story arose out of a casual remark one Bheel made to another in my hearing, as we were passing a certain large tree (with a straight stump about five yards high before the branches began, up which a tiger had jumped) in another part of the country over which I was hunting. Perhaps these dogs hunt the tiger for poaching on their deer, or it may be only the old antipathy between cat and dog, on a large scale.

A man came early on the 28th March to our tent, and told of a tiger he had seen four miles off, so we at once went to the spot, but could nowhere find this beast, although we looked carefully over every likely bit of ground for miles round. Did not get home till late. News of bullocks being killed at "Doraee," six miles off, also reached us at night, so we agreed to hunt there next day.

Early in the morning of the 29th March, having sent on our guns and men, we rode after them, and got to our ground by 9 A.M. Here we were delighted to hear that two tigers were known to live in a deep ravine in the hills near; so we at once, after examining the nature of the cover, decided on posting ourselves at the bottom of one end of the deep ravine, while the beaters went silently round to the other. Almost directly after they had commenced making a noise, we saw a fine tigress moving very cautiously towards us. We let her come close up, without seeing us, when we poured in a volley (one barrel missed fire, so she only got three instead of four bullets). These, however, brought her roaring and charging down past our hiding-place in beautiful style, but so quick that we had no time to exchange our empty rifles for loaded guns before she was out of sight in the high grass beyond. Scarcely had we quickly reloaded, when a magnificent tiger came walking in a most stately manner on to our front. At about twenty yards off he stopped still and stared steadily at us. Being quite ready for him, we at once agreed to open our fire, which was done with good effect; for the tiger began to bound about in all directions, giving us capital opportunities of finishing him, which we did far easier than we had expected, judging from his great size. He measured a few inches over eleven feet, and was exceedingly stout, with an extraordinary quantity of long hair about the face, and even had long curly locks down the back of his neck, much more so than in any we have before or since killed; this greatly added to his personal appearance.

Again loaded, and the beaters having now joined us, we proceeded to look for the first wounded tiger. For this purpose a procession is formed as follows. In front, stooping

Lieut. W. Rice. Del. M & N Hanhart. lith.

ORDER OF PROCESSION FOLLOWING UP A WOUNDED TIGER

down between us, is our head "shikarree," or chief huntsman, who, by carefully observing each footprint or slightest drop of blood, points out the direction in which the wounded game has gone. Keeping guard over him with full cocked rifles, we lead the wedge-shaped procession. Immediately behind us follow our best or steadiest men bearing the spare loaded guns. Next comes the "band," which consists of four or five kettle-drums and one big drum, a man ringing a tremendous bell (novel method of "belling the cat!"), with perhaps others, either blowing a large brass horn, or beating cymbals, besides two of our men constantly loading and firing blank shots from a pair of old horse-pistols. At either side of these are some men armed with drawn swords and two "halberds," or most formidable-looking spears, which serve to keep the beaters well together in passing through high thick grass or reeds, often high over head, for all can see their broad sharp glittering points. Last of all come a number of men engaged in constantly slinging and throwing large stones, which they either pick up as they advance, or take a supply with them before starting, according whether the ground is stony or not. These stones fall just in front, and on all sides of the whole party, often starting a wounded tiger that perhaps would otherwise allow us to pass, in spite even of the deafening noise so close to him. Overlooking all is a man up a tree, which he climbs from time to time as we pass them, keeping a good look-out on all sides for any large game moving ahead. The whole party, in a compact body, keep close together, move at a snail's pace, yell with their utmost power, and create what really is a most infernal din. No tiger will face such a mass of men and noise as this. They sometimes charge down within even a few yards, but then invariably turn off, mostly getting well "peppered," or are shot dead in the attempt.

With this system there is perfect safety to every one, no matter how dense the jungle may be; whereas solitary men or stragglers would be "mauled" to a certainty by the wounded tiger should they attempt to invade the fastness he had sought refuge in.

While thus "following up," there is great difficulty in keeping the men well together, for they seem to consider that every wounded beast must be either already dead or just dying, and so get very careless, and are apt to lag behind unless well looked after. To avoid this noise the wounded tiger will go as far as he possibly can, bleeding often to death before his body is discovered. At other times he will decline moving an inch, roaring awfully at the men from some strong position where he cannot be seen; but a few shots fired at guess seldom fail to start him, so that he can be seen and shot. Sometimes this is easily done by climbing a tree overlooking his retreat. We never had any trouble in persuading men to accompany us after tigers, when they found there was so little danger in so doing; for they seemed to consider the whole business as a good joke. A body of men passing through a cover in this fashion will beat it far more effectually than if drawn out in a long line, for the tiger leaves directly he finds his retreat so disturbed without troubling you to beat every individual bush for him. In some very wide places, or in open plains of high grass, we divided the beaters into two bodies, and so beat over a vast extent of ground at once, each party moving parallel to the other.

In the present case we had not gone above a hundred yards through some very thick jungle, when we were called back by some men in the rear, who said we had passed the tiger. It took us some time to distinguish what they pointed out as the game. It was lying about twenty yards off. We fired together, and instantly down charged the tiger upon us. So thick was the cover that we could not see to fire our second barrels; we merely knew the brute was coming by its roars and the crashing of the bushes. She luckily pulled up just short of us, and again crouched down, being no doubt badly wounded. What she did in the "charge," however, caused a most laughable confusion, for nearly every man of us tumbled down over somebody else, as each, on hearing such roars coming on, involuntarily stepped back a pace. There was a temporary panic, but we soon re-formed and retreated, showing a front to the enemy. After a little delay we advanced again in a different direction, and soon saw the tiger lying down flat under a shady bush, evidently very much done. A few more shots now made the kill secure. We carried both the bodies to our tent, being obliged for some little distance to clear a space among the brushwood with axes, before we could take away this last killed brute, which proved to be a fine tigress. It was dark before we had finished skinning and pegging down the two skins.

Every one seemed much pleased with the day's sport. The large tiger had killed a camel the day before, and had completely gorged himself, but most ungallantly had refused to allow the lady tigress to dine with him, for she was quite empty, although by their footprints of yesterday's date we knew they must both have been together in the same ravine.

During the next three days we were engaged in fruitless searches for tigers reputed to have recently committed great ravages. Bear was all that we could find. On the 2nd April we met and shot a bear. On going up to her, discovered she had two cubs on her back, the usual method with bears of carrying their little ones when too young to save themselves by flight. The little brutes squalled lustily on our nearing them, and at length left their dead mother, whereupon we gave chase, and each caught one alive. Little got a severe bite from his cub in the hand. They were too old to bring up by hand or tame, so the Bheels murdered the little black devils.

Fresh prints of a large tiger were found close to our tent on the 3rd April. We started at once in search of their maker. First searched a "nullah," or small dry water course, full of "corinda" bushes, near at hand. Here Little caught a view of the tiger as he was making off, but out of shot. We now followed up his footsteps for at least two miles, when the ground became too rocky to follow them any longer, so we beat a few patches of cover about, but without success, and returned to again try and follow up the foot-marks. While so doing, we suddenly came most unexpectedly upon this tiger, but he moved off round some rocks before we could get a shot. We now ran hard across an open space about five hundred yards to a ravine, for which he seemed to be making, and got there just in time; for we soon saw him coming quietly towards where we were lying hid, with our spare guns by our side. We allowed him to come within fifteen yards, up to a mark we had agreed should be the signal for firing a volley, when he was at once knocked over; another bullet or two settled him. This tiger measured twelve feet two inches, and was stout in proportion: the largest we had as yet killed.

On the following day, the men we had sent out early to look about for fresh prints of large game, reported that they had found the prints of two tigers, in the bed of a river in which there were some dense covers of "corinda" bushes, willow-trees, and reeds. We tried for a long time to find out where these beasts could be hiding, having beaten the cover, but without seeing them. At length a man thought they must be hid in some very thick "corinda" bushes on the opposite bank of the river, so I waded across the stream, which was about four feet deep, and by carefully looking under the bush, while standing in the water with my rifle all ready, thought I could at last make out what appeared to be part of a tiger, but the bush was so thick and dark that nothing could be distinctly seen, though I was but a very few yards off. On returning to my friend on the opposite bank, we agreed to fire a volley on guess into the bush, so sent all the men well to the rear, to be out of danger. After our first shots all was still, so I fancied that no

tiger could, after all, be in the bush; but presently there was a slight movement, we poured in more shots, and directly afterwards a tiger appeared, which we shot dead by a ball in his skull; the beast fell half in the water down the sloping bank.

Thinking that all the sport was now over, the men, in a body, went round to the dead tiger by a ford higher up the river, and were standing close round it, pointing out to each other the shot-holes, admiring the skin, and talking over its death and the mischief it had done to their cattle, as they usually do, when all of a sudden a most appalling roar was heard to proceed from the very midst of them, as it were. The effect this caused was ludicrous in the extreme, for with one accord they precipitated themselves into the stream with a great splash, and regained the opposite bank in the utmost terror, each struggling to be first across the river. On hearing this roar, all our guns being unloaded at the time, and knowing there must be another tiger close by, we also sought safety in flight. Little got under a bush, while I quickly gained the top of a large thorn-tree nearest me, well scratched in the process, for at the time my costume was extremely scanty, as, on coming out of the water, feeling much chilled, I had taken off my clothes to dry in the sun, and was standing in merely my brown shirt. The next moment we were horrified to hear that a man had been killed. The panic now being over, we reloaded and hastened to the spot, where we were delighted to find that the man was not dead, but had been merely knocked down by a tiger and severely clawed.

It seems that on hearing we had killed the first tiger, this man, who had been posted to look out by himself up a tree, hastened to join the rest of the beaters, while they were rejoicing and talking over the dead tiger. All this time there was another tiger still in the very bush in which we had killed the first one; but as long as the men remained in a body, though only about two yards from them, it kept quite still. On seeing this man approach the bush alone, the beast rushed with loud roars out upon him and knocked him down, actually running off with his turban, which fortunately was a very large one, and no doubt saved his head from the tiger's blows. We had the wounded man at once conveyed to the village, and then tried to follow up the tiger's prints, but could not manage it far, so again began beating some covers about, out of one of which we started the tiger, about fifty yards in our front. He went off at a racing pace; we fired, but apparently missed, and the brute dashed away straight for the hills.

It was too late to look for it there to-day, so we returned to our tent and gave directions for the wounded man to be attended to. After all he seemed more frightened than hurt, excepting some ugly scratches, but he was now quiet enough, having been dosed with quantities of opium, according to native custom in these cases. He soon recovered, and twice afterwards came out hunting with us in following seasons. This accident would never have occurred had he kept close with the other men, for the tigers never attack a large body of people well together, but are sure to select any solitary individual. There was much diving afterwards in the river to recover shields, swords, shoes, spears, and many other articles lost in the panic. The beast we had killed was a fine young tigress. This was the second accident that had happened to our men, but in neither case could we prevent it, nor did we consider ourselves at all to blame, for in both cases they had neglected to observe our most positive caution to keep well together. This we always before starting to hunt took good care to earnestly impress upon the men, and used frequently to send back those who neglected to obey this order, whereby they forfeited part of their day's pay. Before "following up," all old men, or very young ones, were carefully excluded, for they were mostly the offenders, lagging behind either to smoke, or from mere carelessness. Had anybody ever been killed at this sport, we should of course have had to pay his relatives a pension.

Independently of all this, it is a most horrible sickening feeling that comes over you on hearing the cry raised that a man has been killed. Natives are very apt to shout out and repeat this cry on seeing any one covered with blood, when perhaps no very serious damage has been done after all. On one occasion, I remember, when hunting alone, this cry was most needlessly raised; the men began to howl and loudly bewail the supposed loss of one of their number; we had almost cleared a thick patch of willow bushes, through which cover we had beaten without seeing any tiger, though fresh prints were very plentiful, and being so near the end, the Bheels were slightly scattered, when at our very feet up jumped a splendid tiger, and with terrific roars dashed back through the very midst of us into the dense cover we had just been beating. I fired two shots, and afterwards knew he was hit by the quantity of blood we discovered on the bushes. There was at the time some little panic; many nimbly climbed small trees near at hand, while the greater number threw themselves flat on the ground—a capital plan of avoiding danger in these cases. After calling out and answering each other's names, suddenly all began to cry out that one was missing or killed; we supposed he had been carried off by the tiger, for on counting heads over and over again, the proper number of men could not be made up. After a horrible suspense, we were joined by the missing man; the lazy rascal had loitered behind to smoke his pipe. His re-appearance caused a general feeling of intense joy, mingled with anger at the fright he had caused us all, so that we were in doubts whether to almost kiss or kick him.

Next morning, 5th April, we were agreeably surprised with the news that there were fresh prints in the very same cover that we killed yesterday's tigress in. We took up a different position, and again beat the cover; soon a fine tigress came bounding by us at a long gallop. She was instantly rolled over and killed. On inspecting her we were astonished to find that this beast was the same that had escaped us on the previous day. This we knew to be the case by finding two fresh gun-shot wounds on her body—one in the shoulder, and another in the belly; from both these places she had licked off the hair around each wound as large as the palm of a man's hand. We were glad to find these marks, as it proved that we had shot true enough the day before.

CHAPTER VIII.

BUFFALO AND TIGER—AT DINNER—AFTER DINNER—WAITING FOR THE LEAVINGS—TIGER-POISONING—NATIVE POWDER OF LITTLE USE—BULLET WOUNDS—A SHARP ADVENTURE—A LONG CHASE OF AN EPICURE—HUNTED BY A BEAR—A TROUBLESOME BEAST—DEATH OF "WULL."

DURING the next three days we moved only easy stages as far as "Limree," twelve miles, hunting over the whole country on our way, but without finding any large game, although we came upon a bull buffalo just killed.

This we knew must be the work of a very large old male tiger, for we never knew an instance in which a tigress had killed a buffalo unless it was a young or half-grown one. Buffaloes are tremendously powerful animals, and seem almost tiger-proof, unless some solitary straggler is attacked far away from the rest of the herd. When a buffalo is seized by a tiger, all the others immediately come to its rescue, and either drive off the tiger, or cruelly trample upon him and gore him with their hoofs and horns. The men and boys herding buffaloes are well aware of this fact; and, fearlessly seated on the big beasts' back, they do not hesitate to drive them for pasture into any swamp or dense cover, though well aware that tigers also may be lying in the same spot. A herd of buffaloes, coming down to a stream to drink, lie for hours together in the water during the heat of the day, soaking and chewing the cud; their eyes and noses alone visible, perfectly free from all annoyance from the myriads of flies, &c., that would otherwise torment them. I once saw a herd become most excited on smelling the blood of a tiger that I had shot at only a few minutes before, which was plentifully sprinkled on the bushes around. With loud bellowing they at once rushed into the dense cover, crushing down the bushes on all sides, and madly butting with their horns at every thing in their way. The place was so thick, that my men and self were hesitating and wondering what to do, when, to our joy, we saw these cattle coming down to drink. We drove them to the point at which the tiger was last seen to enter the thicket, when, after a good deal of snorting, loud bellows, and pawing the ground, on they rushed with the greatest fury into the close jungle. We followed at a short distance, and found by his blood that the tiger had passed through into another patch of bushes ahead. We left the buffaloes charging and fighting with each other, to the intense disgust of their herdsmen, who had the greatest difficulty to get them all clear of the cover again.

Very different conduct this from that of poor cows, for they scamper off in the greatest alarm, tails up in the air, and heads down, on hearing even the first roar of a tiger, nor do they stop in their headlong flight until far from the scene of their panic. Nor do they assist any unfortunate member of their herd that may have been seized by the tiger. Well knowing where the cattle are daily driven out to graze, the tiger secretes himself in some patch of grass hard by, and waits until they pass his hiding place, when, with a roar, he suddenly starts up, and striking the unlucky bullock with his fore paws about the head, neck, or shoulder, at once fells it to the earth; next, tearing open the victim's throat, he sucks, or laps up rather, the rill of blood that flows fast from the gash or wound his teeth have made. This draught being finished, if undisturbed, he generally retires to some shady bush, a few score yards off, or less, and waits until the cool of the evening, when he creeps out to dine on the beef, invariably beginning his meal at the rump, and so eating up towards the head. Hair, skin, bones, entrails, and meat, all are swallowed in turn. Nor will he cease until about half the bullock has disappeared, except for repeated visits to some piece of water near at hand. While dining, he indulges in a low growling tone of voice. After thus finishing a meal, the tiger will probably lie up in some secluded spot for the next three days, without stirring abroad, except to drink water; until, having well digested his last dinner, his appetite returns.

Almost directly after a bullock has been thus killed, vultures begin to assemble from all points, being somehow soon aware of the "murder" either by their sight or sense of smell, which must be extraordinarily powerful, for, perhaps, not one of these birds will be in sight immediately before the "kill" takes place. Jackals also contrive to be somehow well aware of the fact, for they too begin to assemble on the spot, but both they and the vultures have the good manners to wait until the tiger has quite finished his meal. The vultures sit perched patiently on some neighbouring tree; the jackals sit down at a respectful distance. After the tiger has dined, there is a regular scramble for the remaining portion of the dead bullock, the jackals chasing away and jumping up at the vultures, as they swoop past them whilst trying to filch some scrap of meat or entrails, in the most ridiculous style. Somehow the birds always contrive to avoid the vicious snaps made at them by the jackals. These curs having, perhaps, each retired with some bone to gnaw at leisure, the vultures begin in earnest, soon completely clearing up every shred of meat, leaving the bones beautifully picked. After such a feast, they are often so gorged, as to be utterly unable to rise or fly away.

The cowherds often revenge themselves in a very clever way upon the tiger. Being well aware of his habit of beginning to dine at the rump of the slaughtered ox, directly he leaves the body on having drank the last drop of its blood, the herdsman, who has perhaps been watching his proceedings from some tree close by, quietly descends, and with his knife cuts several long gashes in the dead bullock's hind quarters. In these wounds he rubs or places a quantity of powdered arsenic, as well as the flour of a certain red berry pounded fine, which grows common enough in all large jungles. Either of these poisons will answer his purpose, being nearly tasteless. As usual, the tiger comes out of his retreat at dusk, to dine, and he insensibly swallows a quantity of the poison with each mouthful of meat. This creates excessive thirst, so that he betakes himself to the nearest stream, which he seldom leaves, drinking until he almost seems fit to burst, then dies.

To my great annoyance, an old cowherd once showed me with great glee how he managed to thus be even with his enemies the tigers. Three of these beasts he had lately poisoned, and their remains were to be seen at three separate pools of water, within a circle of as many miles. Of course, as a tiger-hunter, I was obliged to appear delighted with his success, while the loss of sport he had caused, much grieved me.

Again, it is a common custom when a tiger has killed a bullock for the owners at once to make a platform of branches placed across each other high up in some tree overlooking the dead ox, and here quietly wait with a loaded matchlock until the tiger makes his appearance in the evening, when they can safely get a good shot at him. They very rarely manage to kill the tiger dead, for the bullet used is very small; but if he is merely wounded there is a great chance of the tiger afterwards soon dying, for the wound gets full of maggots in a very short time, owing to the swarms of flies about. Yet they do recover occasionally from these wounds, for we have several times on skinning a tiger cut out old matchlock-balls that have long been embedded in his body, mostly very little below the surface. With bears, it was a very common thing indeed to find these bullets merely skin deep. The bears most likely were shot by men watching their fields at night to keep off hog, for whole droves of pig come out of the adjoining jungles and create fearful havoc in the corn and sugar-cane fields, in spite even of repeated shots and the shouts of the husbandmen.

Native gunpowder is very coarse and bad, which accounts for the bullets having so little effect on such tough brutes as bears. Even our own shots seldom passed clean through the body of these animals, for on skinning them we used often to find our bullets much flattened sticking against the skin on the opposite side to that at which they had entered the beast we had fired at. These were all recent shots, for we never, except once, ever killed either a tiger or bear that seemed to have recovered from wounds received from our guns, or discovered in their bodies any of our bullets of long standing; so that in point of fact every animal recorded as being merely wounded might with equal truth be counted as killed. This single exception was a tigress that had a bullet completely flattened buried just under the skin in her chest, where it had been lodged plainly for some long time. This ball had evidently first struck a stone and then rebounded on the tigress, causing but a very slight wound. From its size it was clearly no matchlock-ball, but where we killed this tigress we had not before wounded one, so that if the ball was ours she must have travelled a long distance.

Having sent on our baggage to "Limree," we rode across country, the 9th of April, to beat a famous cover we had heard of at about three miles' distance. On arriving at the ground, we discovered that this place was merely a branch or continuation of the splendid ravine called "Kokee." There were a number of vultures about, so we knew some animal had lately been killed by wild beasts. On beating this cover the men soon started a very large tiger, but the brute declined to be driven at any price in the direction we wished—stood his ground, and roared awfully at the men; so we left our position to take up another, in the hope that this tiger would have no objection to break cover in another quarter. For this purpose, taking three Bheels with us to carry the spare guns and water-bag, we were in the act of crossing round by the upper end of the ravine, when one of the men suddenly gave their usual warning note of danger—a sharp short whistle. He most luckily had caught sight of a tiger lying asleep among some high shady green rushes exactly in our path. Little, who was in advance, had almost stepped on this beast, without being aware of its presence. We quickly and silently retired a few steps up a bank overlooking the patch of reeds; here, placing the spare guns at our feet, and having sent the men to the rear, we at once commenced firing at the sleeping beauty. Up she jumped with terrible roars on being so rudely awakened, but our shots fell so quick that she never properly got her legs before being again and again upset. We saw at once that she was ours, and a few more balls finished her. We were only seven or eight yards from her, so it was impossible to miss a single shot.

This beast had been lying in a beautifully cool place, for a small stream flowed through the thick shady patch of green reeds in which she had chosen to sleep, and her skin was wet on one side. We again tried to drive out the old tiger we first had hunted, but it was still impossible to make him show himself; so we returned and skinned the one we had just killed on the spot. It was a fine tigress, and very prettily marked. After this troublesome job we rode for our tent across country, and got there by dark.

Fresh prints of a tiger having been found about a mile from our tent, on the 10th, we set out to look for their owner, beating all day long several thick detached patches of jungle in the bed of the river, which was then almost dry. At length our men started this tiger out of some high grass, at least six miles from where we first began looking for this brute, although we constantly found his fresh prints in the covers we had just beaten, which proved that he must have been moving about since the previous night. We did not see this tiger, unluckily, for it was getting cool when he was at last found, and he made off across an open space far from where we were posted. Just before the men found him he had killed a cow heavy with calf, and merely drank her blood and then decamped. The marks of his claws where he had struck his victim on the neck were very visible, and extended over a great space, showing how wide open the tiger's paw must stretch on his striking a blow. This beast was well known and much hated for the number of cattle he killed and wasted. Having once been clumsily fired at and only slightly wounded by a man who had watched for him from a tree over the dead body of a bullock he had just killed, this beast had ever afterwards made a practice of merely drinking the blood of the cattle he destroyed without ever again visiting their dead bodies to eat up the meat. In this wasteful manner he sometimes at different places killed several cows in the same day. Going homewards we shot a couple of "cheetul" deer for the beaters to eat; and did not get back till late and after dark.

The next morning we started early to beat "Kokee" ravine, three miles from our tent. While going ahead of the men to take up our position, we unexpectedly came upon a tigress with three half-grown cubs. We fired and wounded the old one, when she instantly disappeared in the thick jungle. We next turned our attention to the three cubs, who seemed too much astonished at the row that was going on to follow their mother's example. We wounded all three, but only got one; for we did not like to enter such a thicket, knowing there were three other wounded tigers in it at the time. We tried all day to drive out the tigress alone by throwing stones and firing shots at guess into the cover, but she would not leave her young ones. Twice or thrice we caught a view of her, merely for a moment, as she tried to induce them to follow her higher up the ravine, by going ahead and calling to them; but we could not fire.

We went to look on the next day for this wounded tigress, which we supposed would have retreated to another ravine after the treatment she had received at this place. On looking down into the deep ravine from the edge of a precipice which formed one of its sides, we spied a large tiger moving off quickly below us. We fired, but the distance was too great. On hearing our shots at this tiger, a bear turned out of his cave just opposite, so we gave him also a few shots; but then, having nobler game in view, hastened after the big tiger. After running as hard as we could for more than half a mile in the hope of heading the tiger, Little pulled up on hearing some monkeys "swear," and, on looking over the edge of the precipice along which we had been running, saw the tiger about ten yards off, moving slowly immediately below him. He instantly planted a ball between the brute's shoulders, which rolled him over without a groan. We fired another shot or two to make sure, but they were unnecessary. After first firing at this tiger, and in the excitement of the subsequent chase, we had forgotten all about the bear we had hit on his turning out so close to us, but now the men loudly called after us that he too was following our way. We looked round, and sure enough there was the bear coming on, now only about forty yards off; we walked forward to meet him, and gave him four balls, whereupon he rose on his hind legs perfectly upright, and seizing a small tree in his confusion, shook it violently until it snapped, when he fell backwards; but afterwards recovering his legs, tried to bolt back, we after him, loading and firing as quickly as possible. At last, after many shots, he also was bagged. Neither of us had ever before seen such a large bear, or one that so easily carried so much lead. He was a perfect monster, and evidently very old; one of his tusks was broken,

SLAUGHTERING A GIGANTIC BEAR.

and two others completely worn down level with his jaw, The tiger, too, was a fine one, measuring eleven feet six inches, and very stout. We sent for one of our camels, and had both the bodies carried to our tent, where we skinned and pegged them down by sunset. At first the camel objected to carry such a novel burden, but, by binding a cloth over his eyes, and coaxing him a little, we managed to sling the game on either side, and start homewards, much pleased with the day's sport.

Early on the following morning we went after the tigress we had wounded on the 11th April, and saw her, but far out of range, as she was going over a steep hill with only one cub with her; the other, no doubt, had died of his wounds in the meantime. We followed up, and again started either this tiger or another (for there was no cub with her then), at which I could only get a shot as it was walking off. My bullet struck somewhere about the brute's hind-quarters, and caused it to roar. It was too late in the day to attempt following up this tiger any longer. On the 14th we made one more effort to kill the tigress we had been hunting for the last three days. We soon found her in the same place; but by this time she was very cautious, for she moved very slowly, stopping at almost every step to stare about her. At last she discovered where we were lying down flat on a bank, and was taking a long steady look to more clearly make us out, when I was obliged to fire. The ball struck her in the throat or chest; and on she came at a great pace with loud roars, and rushed past us through the thick cover for another dense patch of jungle beyond. We could not see to get another shot at this time, but shortly afterwards Little caught sight of her drinking at a small pool of water on the borders of the thicket in which she had pulled up. The rings on the water, caused by her tongue while silently lapping, first drew his attention to her whereabouts. He quickly gave her a ball in the ribs, whereupon she sprang back into the cover. Into this patch of jungle we threw volleys of large stones, besides firing several shots on guess, but could nowhere discover the tigress; so, first placing some men up trees all round to look out, we advanced in a body into the thicket, making our utmost noise. After going about half way through this, the tigress, with terrible roars, jumped up at our very feet, and bolted back for the cover out of which we had first started her. The bushes were so thick and close that we never even saw her, although certainly not more than three paces from us at the time we put her out of this last hiding place, which was between two rocks. These, perhaps, shielded her from our random shots, and the showers of stones we had pitched into this patch of jungle. There was a great quantity of blood about, so we felt sure she must soon die. Obliged now to go home, on account of its getting too dark to hunt for her any longer.

While lying down hid on the bank to-day, before this tiger showed herself, three large bears passed close by above us, but we did not fire, for they did not seem to observe us. Before leaving this part of the country, we paid the bear we had disturbed on the 13th April a visit, and again saw him, but could only get long shots as he bolted off, one or two of which caused him to loudly growl.

Thinking we should perhaps be able to find the tigress we had so repeatedly shot at, either dead or dying, in the long "Kokee" ravine, I took out my three dogs—two greyhounds and poor "Wull"—to assist in the search. Here, sad to tell, from some unaccountable cause, poor "Wull" tumbled over the edge of a precipice and cracked his skull. He must have died instantly. We did not discover the tigress.

CHAPTER IX.

CHANGE OF QUARTERS—BLUE BULL—ORDER OF MARCH—WORK IN CAMP—ADVICE TO SPORTSMEN—FISH-SHOOTING—THE JUNGLE A LIVING LARDER—VERY VARIOUS SPORT—A BHEEL EXPOSED TO DIE—NATIVE SUPERSTITIONS.

WE now changed our quarters, and from "Limree" marched to "Ambah," but found no large game. The kit was sent on to "Chuldoo," another short march of six miles, but still nothing worth firing at was seen. On the road, as usual, we got shots at "chinkara" (gazelles). These small deer are common enough in all open places, and are not bad eating, so we mostly looked out for them for the pot, or else perhaps a shot could be had at some old blue bull, as he stood stupidly staring at our retinue on the march. Our strange procession seemed to puzzle these animals, for they would sometimes look on at us quite tamely, until perhaps a ball in tho forehead would drop the leader of the herd, when the rest of the wild cows would canter off. We only shot these mild creatures for the beaters to eat. They used to cut off the flesh in long strips, and hang these on boughs to dry in the sun all round our little encampment, which by no means added to its appearance, giving it much the look of the "shambles." This meat, thus dried, will keep for a long time, but the process is not savoury.

On determining to change our ground, to hunt over another part of the country, a very busy scene would take place. Striking the small tents, of which we carried two, one being for the servants, and the other for ourselves, more to keep our goods in than to live in, unless heavy rain happened to fall—for we always preferred sleeping and dining out in the open air—

and packing up in deal boxes an infinite number of all sorts of articles, these would soon be divided into equal loads, and placed on the camels' backs. All being at length ready, mounting our horses, off we started, leaving the dogs and goats to follow of their own accord. First came some men carrying our guns and the water bag; these acted as guides to show the way, and were very useful in assisting us to get other men at the different villages we passed through, or thought it worth while to halt at, according to the prospect of sport there was in the neighbourhood. On thus providing their substitutes, we sent them back to their homes well pleased with a liberal payment for their services, for these men would be perfectly useless over a country with which they were unacquainted; besides, after a few days' hunting, they seemed anxious to attend to their fields and cattle, so would not stay. We rode slowly in advance, looking out for any sort of deer that might be found feeding on the roadside. Next came our spare horses, led by their grooms. Then the camels, following each other, surrounded by our servants, who either rode small ponies or the camels, or walked on foot. The washermen, as usual, mounted their bullocks. On reaching our halting ground, the first thing was to select some large shady trees to pitch the tent under, where there was plenty of water near at hand, not neglecting to see whether any bees had formed their nests overhead in the trees; for, on two or three occasions, from omitting this precaution, we suffered severely from the bees that were disturbed by the smoke arising from our cooking fires. Our little encampment was often quite picturesque; with the horses and ponies picketed in a row, while the servants, camels, bullocks, goats, dogs, and fowls, were grouped around. Bright wood-fires for cooking added to the scene, which never looked so well in our opinion as when there were several skins stretched out, and pegged down, just before the tent.

This tiresome work, as well as the troublesome one of

skinning the "large game," we always performed ourselves, assisted by our "huntsmen," for we found if the business was left to others, that great lumps of meat would be carelessly left on the skins, besides many ugly cuts from knives. In the same manner the skin would be pegged down in any shape, and so spoilt. From long practice we became very expert in these operations, which, however, are anything but pleasant, especially with blunt knives, or bad pegs, when many severe raps on the fingers are often the consequence. However the trouble was well repaid when at last a coating of arsenical soap to preserve the skins had been rubbed in, and we were at leisure to admire our work over some "mug" (a delicious refreshing beverage composed of beer, spice, sugar and water), and talk over the last "kill," with the chances of the next.

On 19th April, we went with a good many men to beat a cover in which we had last year killed a tiger. Presently a tiger was seen going up a bank, but at least 130 yards from our post. I fired one shot, and luckily broke her fore arm, whereupon she came down roaring straight towards us, holding up the broken leg. On nearing us she was quickly killed. Two half-grown cubs, the men assured us, had broken back past them while beating this cover, so we looked for them in all the likely places about, but without finding them.

Having marched towards "Bhynsoreghur," we pitched our tent in a very jungly spot on the banks of a small river. Herds of "cheetul" deer came down to drink quite close to our tent in the morning and evening, but we did not fire at these, for fear of disturbing the country we had yet to hunt over.

On arriving at new ground, we made it a rule to abstain, as much as possible, from firing at any small game, unless it was absolutely required for the pot; when we shot either a few green wood-pigeons (flocks of which were everywhere to be found in all large forests), or a hare, which, by turning out all hands to beat the bushes, was generally to be got within a few yards of our camp, or a "murrel" fish. Many a chance of finding large game has been lost by sportsmen attempting to thus combine a search for small game, such as "sambur" and "cheetul," in the cool of the morning, intending to hunt for nobler game in the heat of the day. However pleasant and tempting it may be, while merely strolling a short distance before breakfast, to knock over a fine pair of horns, which, when "pitched" in the jungle, may be often got within a few yards of the tent even, still the practice had best be avoided; for this is the very time at which bears and tigers, after having been prowling about all night long, are returning to their respective lairs, to lie up for the rest of the day. On hearing shots in their neighbourhood, which, perhaps, has not been so disturbed throughout the rest of the year, they naturally betake themselves to other covers a few miles off, well knowing that such an unusual noise clearly shows the presence of their great enemy, the hunter, who, to his surprise, on visiting all the most likely places about, during the hottest time of the day, can find nothing but prints. He curses his bad luck, and wonders why the beast, of all the days in the year, should have chosen that particular one to sleep out; and he moves on to hunt over fresh ground, when the game he has thus passed over quietly returns to its accustomed haunts.

Talking of shooting fish sounds rather strange in England, but in India it is a very common practice, and is thus managed. Taking his matchlock, the native quietly secretes himself on some bank or tree overlooking any river, or lake, in which "murrel" fish are plentiful. He avoids being dressed in white clothes, or making the slightest movement or noise, otherwise the fish will not rise. After waiting quite still some little time his patience is rewarded by a fine "murrel" (a species of large fresh-water carp) quietly rising to the top of the water to breathe, for having emitted one bubble of air it generally as gradually begins to descend, repeating this process at intervals of every five minutes or so. This is the lucky moment to seize for a shot at the fish's head. No sooner has the ball struck the water than with a great splash of its tail the fish disappears; hastily throwing down his gun, the marksman instantly dives in after the fish, and begins groping about with his hands and legs in all directions round the spot where the fish has last gone down, until he is able to feel it, mostly lying stunned and motionless among the weeds at the bottom. Having grasped it, he rises with his slippery prize, and flings it far on to the shore, for it soon recovers itself, and if not found at once on diving for it, the fish would swim away. These "murrel" are excellent eating, very firm and white, and of a most delicate flavour. They often reach even three feet long, by about six inches broad. While lying motionless at the top of the water they look like mere black logs of floating wood, often merely the nose is to be seen, as the fish hides under some large water-lily leaf, so that a sharp look-out must be kept. It is immaterial whether the bullet actually strikes the fish or not; if it goes very near its head or mouth it will have just the same effect of stunning the "murrel." I have myself, for fun, in about a quarter of an hour's time, shot at, dived for, and brought ashore three monster fish of this carp breed, not one of which bore any marks of the bullets. This fact the Bheels laughably accounted for by saying, that on opening its mouth to breathe, the fish accidentally gulps down a mouthful of water, which has been rendered perfectly boiling for the moment by the rapid course of the ball through it, the novel taste of swallowing which so confuses the "murrel" that it forgets how to escape. Nor could they understand how the fish could possibly be stunned, unless actually hit by the bullet, water being too soft for the purpose.

The sportsman has but little fear of starving in the woods, where nature has so abundantly provided food, even if the natives refuse to furnish any sort of supplies, as was sometimes our case, when even a kid could not be procured from their numerous flocks for four times its value, solely from motives of opposition or disinclination to oblige, for which we were puzzled to account. Besides deer of all sorts, hog, hares, partridges, jungle-fowl, fish, peacocks, and pigeons, literally abound; but these latter birds, though very good eating, we refrained from shooting, as they are both regarded with veneration by the natives of this part of the country from some superstitious notions or other. Luxuries even were to be had, for scarcely a day passed but what a honey-comb was found by the beaters, and presented to us. After having beaten two large patches of willow cover in the bed of the river, without success, we took up our position to try at a third. We invariably remained alone at any position we had chosen to take up, as it seemed utterly impossible for most of the men we had tried, on allowing them to remain with us, to keep quiet on seeing any wild beast approach our post, whereby the animal was sure to discover our whereabouts, and escape before a shot could be obtained, greatly to our annoyance. The men, suddenly hearing a low growl in a bush by which they were passing, at once returned to us with the news.

We accordingly changed our ground, and the beating began. First, a half-grown tiger made its appearance, closely followed by another of the same size. One was quickly laid low, and the other made off badly wounded. Presently, a terrific roar was heard from the very same patch of jungle, out of which these young ones had broken. By this, we knew that their mother was also there, and shortly after she bounded out, but at too great a distance for our double guns (the rifles being now unloaded). We fired and hit her, but she went off. We now followed up the blood and prints of the first wounded young tiger, and soon despatched him. We now returned to our tent, not liking to try again for the old tigress we had so slightly wounded, for, having seen her family murdered, she was sorely enraged, and might have charged our men, who could scarcely keep close enough in such a very dense cover. At night this tigress kept us all awake for a long time, by roaring close to our encampment, much to the annoyance of our servants and horses. She was evidently calling for her young ones. More wood was piled on all the fires around, and a few blank pistol-shots fired, but she still remained.

On the 25th, we beat the same ground, at which we yesterday commenced hunting, and put up two bears, but did not fire at them, for the men had disturbed a very knowing tiger, that would not move at all, but roared awfully at the beaters whenever they approached his hiding place. We accordingly stopped the beating noise, and changed our position, hoping to drive him past in another direction; but here we soon after saw the tiger quietly trying to sneak out of the cover, even before the men had recommenced making another attempt to drive him out. We fired, and wounded him severely, with three shots. Afterwards, we followed up the blood for some distance over very bushy ground, until it most unaccountably entirely ceased; so we lost this tiger, which was a very fine one, with a dark coloured skin.

On the 26th, we went in search of the tigress we wounded on the 24th; and again put her up in the same cover as before, but could not see to fire at her, as she broke back past the beaters, making a fearful row, so much so that we greatly feared some accident had happened. Luckily the men were well together when she raced past them. The tigers in this part of the country had been much bullied by a native prince, who lived at the Fort of "Bhynsrode," but he did not seem able, judging from their numbers, to kill them, although using elephants for the purpose; for we found the different covers about full of elephants' marks. After being hunted by elephants, the tigers may perhaps despise the efforts of men to turn them out of their fastnesses, for we found the beasts here very unwilling to move.

Marched on the 27th to "Amtee Amlee," seven miles. Going along, we beat a ravine on the right of the road, and put out a tiger, which we quickly knocked over dead. Then tried another patch of jungle close by, but saw nothing. On returning, a tiger was viewed by the men making for the very cover in which we had just killed one, so we reached our old position by a circuitous route, and again beat this place, but without finding this other tiger. He must have passed on, although we lost no time in looking him up. Got to our tent by sunset, being late in consequence of stopping to skin the dead tiger on the spot. While so doing, we discovered a number of porcupine quills in his feet, arms, and even face. These broken pieces of quill we had also met with on other occasions when skinning tigers, which proves that they must be fond of such food. The porcupine only feeds at night, when, doubtless, the tiger often meets him, and, with a gentle tap of his paw, destroys him, in spite of his armour of quills.

While beating one of the covers to-day, our men found a poor Bheel lying near some water under a rocky ledge here; he had been left out to die, being very weak and ill, by his companions, far away from any village or habitation. One of the tigers we were after passed close by this man and roared at him, but did not hurt him. We tried to persuade the men to carry him home, but this he himself did not wish to be done; so we left him behind, wondering rather at such a strange custom.

During the next four days, we marched along the river "Chumbul," as far as the village of "Manowlee," but found no game, except deer, worth firing at, until we reached "Ranee ka Rora," a small village on the other bank of the river, which we crossed in a ferry-boat; and sent the camels a long way round to a ford, for the river is very wide at this part.

Here an old man told of a tiger that had killed several of his cattle. Without some such provocation we found the people of this country very unwilling to inform against the tigers, or even to admit that such animals existed at all in their neighbourhood. This, no doubt, partly arises from a superstitious idea they have that, if merely wounded, the tiger or his relations will revenge himself either on them or their cattle. Besides, many sects consider the tiger rather a sacred beast than otherwise, and would only wish to have them destroyed in the event of the tiger turning "man-eater;" a breach of faith towards his worshippers not to be pardoned. This is the same religious sort of feeling, originating in dread, that causes the natives not to molest the most venomous snakes.

Collecting about twenty men we set off for a beautiful shady cover, full of high green reeds, "corinda" bushes, and willow trees, called "ambah," about three miles from our halting-place. Here, on the beating having begun, we at once felt sure that some large game was in the cover; for the monkeys about kept up a great noise. Presently I saw a tigress approach our position, and then stop short to take a long stare at us at about twelve yards off. We were obliged to fire at once. The ball hit her somewhere about the head, when, with a roar, she turned back into the thick jungle. Soon after we saw this tigress trying to break out of the cover by going over a low bank at one side. A shot now brought her down charging towards us in splendid style—tail up, mouth open, claws out, and roaring loudly—from about sixty yards. But by this move she merely committed suicide, for two more shots rolled her over, and a few more quite settled her. We took off the skin there and then, and got back to the tent by dark, all well pleased.

CHAPTER X.

Bad luck—An astonishing leap—Three in a cave—A running fight with a bear—A stiff chase—Wounded panther—A tiger's tracks—Ignorance of the natives—Wounded tigers do not always bleed—Various fortune—Beware of the bees!—In hospital.

During the next two days, we hunted over a good deal of ground, and discovered the footprints of two or three tigers; but in a country abounding in rocks, caves, and water, and unfavourable for sport because without bushes. But on the 4th of May, while beating through a ravine near "Dowd," we were gladdened by the sight of a fine tiger. He came straight towards the point we had chosen to guard—a bank overlooking the open ravine. Every now and then this tiger stopped to listen attentively to the beaters. When he was in the act of passing us about twenty yards off, I fired, perhaps a little too soon; but the ball passed clean through his skull and dropped him instantly. My comrade gave him another shot as he moved slightly in his dying agony, when he was quiet enough.

During the succeeding five days, we moved through the country diligently searching for game, finding tracks of tigers, bears, and panthers; but failing to discover the beasts themselves.

On the 9th of May, we determined to beat the whole of a ravine named "Indoreghur," near the large city of "Bhampoora." Here there is capital cover of willow bushes, rocks, and caves, with a clear stream running from end to end through the place. Rather to our surprise, the whole jungle proved empty. We had consequently returned to our tent, but had scarcely been back five minutes when a man came running to tell us that he had seen a tiger try to creep out of a thick patch of cover between two steep hills that we had already beaten. This beast had cunningly remained hidden, in spite of the noise of the men; but thinking the danger over, he was attempting to sneak off unobserved to some distant jungle, when this man, whom we had placed on the look-out, luckily happened to loiter behind a little, and so saw the tiger. On hearing this good news, we hastily resumed our former position on the sloping side of a hill, and sent the beaters round to again drive this cover by rolling down large stones from the steep hills above. Presently a fine tigress came bounding by at a great pace about seventy yards in our front; we fired both our double rifles, and one shot from a gun, but she continued her rapid course for about a hundred yards, when she suddenly made a tremendous spring in the air, clearing a small tree in her path, over seven feet high, and fell dead on the other side. We measured this leap, which was over seven yards from where she had last touched the ground, or "taken off." We found blood on the topmost boughs of the small tree. She seemed to drop dead in the air. This tigress was very old, and had one tusk broken. On taking off her skin, we discovered some small pieces of lead under it, so she had doubtless been fired at before, which taught her to behave so cunningly.

On the 12th May, after beating a very thick cover close to the village of "Gole Amba," which, to our surprise, turned out a blank, we were directed to station ourselves above the low hills, immediately over a cave, for which the men assured us a tiger, if started, would make. They commenced beating along the foot of the hills from a long distance. A fine buck sambur, with splendid horns, turned out of the cover below us, and just as we had decided from this fact that no large game would be lying in the same jungle, out bolted a tiger at our very feet, from the cave over which we were keeping guard. He made straight towards three Bheels near, who somehow, without our knowledge, had thus managed to misplace themselves, in the hope of seeing the sport. We did not dare fire, for fear of either hurting these men, or of turning the tiger on to them, but loudly called out and warned them of their danger. With admirable presence of mind, they at once began to bawl out as loud as possible, and continued throwing showers of stones before them; these luckily turned off the tiger as soon as he appeared in sight of the three men, for he swerved from his course past them with loud roars, and made off for another patch of jungle, about half a mile further on. Seeing from our high post the point he was making for, we ran along the hill top at our utmost speed, and presently saw him, but very indistinctly, on account of the dense bushes coming straight towards us. Suddenly we heard a loud roar, which we fancied at the time was caused by his disgust at again viewing us, but the real cause was soon explained. On his showing himself, I dropped him with a lucky shot through the shoulders at about seventy yards' distance, while Little gave a few more shots to make sure. Then, to our surprise, two large bears turned out close by him. We instantly opened fire on these brutes also; one fell dead, and the other bolted off, growling terribly, among some extremely dense thorn-bushes in the plain below. We gave chase, but soon lost this wounded bear, although there was plenty of blood to be seen for a long way. The tiger had evidently meant to lie up in the shade of a cave which was already occupied by these bears. They would not turn out for him, in spite of his roars; he had to seek another retreat, in looking for which he exposed himself, and so got killed. We sent for a camel, and had both the dead bear and tiger, as on a former occasion, carried to our tent, where we could skin them in the shade at our leisure.

On the 14th, we sent the tent on to the small village of "Goola," eight miles, but remained behind ourselves to look for a tiger, whose fresh prints I had discovered within a few hundred yards of our encampment. We followed up these tracks a long way into the hills, and beat two covers there, but without starting the game; so again went to keep watch over the cave out of which a tiger had bolted on the 12th May. The men had quite finished beating all the remaining cover at the foot of the hill, and we fancied no chance of sport was left, when as a last hope we threw a good many stones into the mouth of the cave, and were about to leave the place, when most unexpectedly a fine tigress rushed at full speed out of the den. We let her get clear of some trees, and then fired, but she still continued going off, roaring all the while, until some lucky long shot or other caused her to stop short in a patch of high grass. We went up to the spot, and found her dead. Rode on to "Goola" by sunset, rejoicing at our good luck.

We beat the steep hills here overlooking the river "Chumbul," as far as the point on which the fort of "Shanghur" or "Chourassa" is built, but without finding any large game. Plenty of sambur were started, but at these we did not fire. Returning to our tent, we spied a large bear asleep in a cave; we fired together and wounded him, but he disappeared still farther into the den; presently, to our surprise, we again caught sight of him moving off at about eighty yards' distance, having emerged from the mass of broken rocks that formed the hill side at another point, travelling underground to this other mouth of the cave. We again fired and brought him round on us sharp, but finding the shots too many, he turned off and tried to run away. We gave chase, and though he made several clumsy attempts at charging, was soon killed. The men carrying our spare guns did not at all like his looks or loud growls, so kept well behind out of danger; so we had to reload as we ran, and after firing, it was often our turn to retreat. The rest of the beaters now came up and told us that on our first firing at the bear a large tiger had turned out of a cave about twenty yards from where they were following us, having evidently been disturbed by the noise of our shots. The men all quickly climbed up trees, and the tiger moved off. We hastened to the spot, and soon I caught an indistinct view of the tiger about 150 yards distant, as he slowly walked through some very thick thorn-bushes in the direction the men had pointed out. I fired one shot, but it was not answered by the usual half-grunt, half-roar sort of noise tigers generally utter on being struck. Nor could we again see the brute. It was now getting too cool and late to attempt hunting up this tiger, so we left him for the next day, and walked home to our camp, bringing the bear on a small tree with us to skin there.

Next morning we went to look for yesterday's tiger, and put him out of the same place, but he kept in the midst of the thickest part of the jungle, so we could only get a view of him now and then by running along the top of the rocky cliff overlooking this cover. We fired several shots at him as he moved on below us at least 150 yards off. This we continued doing for nearly two miles, reloading as we ran on ahead to get a fresh shot. At last a lucky bullet caused him to suddenly stop under a shady tree among some high green rushes on the bank of the river "Chumbul." Having placed some men to look out and see that he did not still move on, we went down to find our game, first sending two men across to a small island or sandbank in the middle of the river, opposite the thick cover in which the tiger had pulled up. These men soon called out for us to follow them, for they had seen the tiger from their post. We, hastily taking off our heavy boots, &c., were in the act of wading across to the island when we saw the tiger slowly creeping down to the water's edge to drink, his wounds and such a long walk in the sun having, no doubt, made him feel thirsty. We quickly gave him more lead, when he sprang back out of sight into the thick bushes. Here we continued firing from the sand-bank at least thirty more shots when all was still. On cautiously approaching the place we found the tiger dead with many balls in him. He measured eleven feet eleven inches, and was exceedingly stout. We had fully two hours' hard work to kill this beast, so after skinning him on the spot returned to the tent by 4 P.M.

While walking along the top of some hills on the 17th, we suddenly put out a panther from a cave a little below us. Two shots hit this brute, one breaking his hind leg as he bolted off. This caused the panther to stop under every little shady bush he passed in the plain below, until at last we marked him down under a shady tree. Placing men all round on the hills above to keep watch, we now went down to finish this wounded animal, but were disappointed, for he had managed to walk off without being discovered by the men on the look out. There was plenty of blood about, and we tracked him a good distance, but without again finding the beast. We afterwards rode on to the village of "Kona," four miles, in the evening, the tent having been sent on there.

At this place we could not hear of any tigers, so we beat along the hills on speculation. Suddenly we came upon a bear with a young one near a large cave. The mother was shot dead directly, but we spared the young one until he should grow bigger; he was quite old enough to find his own living. Going homewards, another large bear was started; we rolled him over twice, but he made off at such a pace, that it was useless to think of overtaking him. The villagers at this place seemed astonished at our display of tiger and bear skins which we unrolled and spread out to dry.

We moved our camp to "Booj," a village six miles distant, on the 19th. While riding there we found fresh prints of an enormous tiger on the road, along which he had been walking for some distance, every now and then rolling himself in the fine dust, as is the custom with these animals in the hot weather. This they do, according to the Bheels' account, to free themselves of the small insects with which they are sometimes troubled, (a species of sheep-tick.) He also left long marks by the roadside, where he had scratched up the earth with his hind legs, as a dog sometimes does. Unfortunately all our guns had been sent on ahead with our men, who had gone on to collect other beaters at "Booj," and announce our coming, so we could not follow up this tiger's prints.

We were obliged to often thus send on our men early to any distant part we had determined to hunt over, otherwise the men of that particular neighbourhood would have all left for their several duties for the day; some to watch their cattle, while grazing in the jungle, others to cut wood, attend to their fields, or look for gum and honey in the forests. Unless we could secure the attendance of some of the people of the place, who are well acquainted with the most likely spots in which large game would be found, it would have been a mere waste of time to attempt hunting for tigers or bears in any direction, trusting to chance alone whether we happened to discover their hiding-places.

It was astonishing how ignorant the inhabitants of this part of the country seemed to be of the ground only a few miles from their own homes. This is accounted for by the fact that very many of them have passed their whole lives without ever having wandered even ten miles from their own villages. Nor could we induce them by any reward to accompany us any distance, for only two or three days' time, from their own neighbourhood to assist us in hunting. When travelling, fresh guides had to be taken from every village on the road, each pretending that he was unacquainted with the way any further on. If we intended to ride on after our men at a faster pace

M & N Hanhart, Lith.

BOOJ TIGER.

than the guides on foot could travel, we always directed our servants to pile up four stones, pyramid fashion, at the side of the path they had taken. This saved all doubt on coming to either cross roads or where several paths diverged, as to which was the right one. Nor did we ever lose our way by adopting this simple method, when otherwise, on stony ground, we should have been greatly puzzled, and might have looked in vain for any one to direct us. To lose one's way in the jungle is a very easy feat, but decidedly unpleasant, with a tired horse to watch, no dinner, and the ground for your bed all the night.

On arriving at "Booj," we beat the beautiful cover of willow bushes and high reeds there in the bed of the river, out of which the men started both a tiger and bear; but unfortunately we saw neither of these animals, being wrongly placed. Next day we again tried the same cover, but it was empty. Presently we saw some fresh prints of a tiger leading to a small ravine or branch of the river here, so went ahead with our spare guns while the men began beating up towards us. Soon a Bheel came running to say that they had started the tiger, but that it had at once left this cover and gone across an open plain to another patch of jungle close by. We directly went there, and after throwing in several volleys of large stones out rushed the tiger within three or four yards only of where we were standing; but the cover was unluckily so thick that we could not clearly see the brute. We fired, but could not tell for certain whether the tiger was hit or not. The ground was much too stony to be able to follow up its prints far, nor could we find any blood about, in spite of the six or eight shots we fired; so we could not consider this tiger even wounded. It several times happened, especially if the game was going at any great pace, that we did not at the time find blood, although the animal was severely wounded or even found dead after following up its footprints for some little distance. This is easily to be understood when it is remembered that the loose skin of the tiger being stretched by the animal's great exertions as it either bounds off in a series of tremendous leaps, or races by at its utmost speed, may not then cover the exact part of the body that it would on the beast resuming its usual state of repose, when a wound would very likely be hidden under sound skin; and it would take some little time for the blood from such a shot to trickle or find its way out of the bullet-hole in the skin, which might be several inches away from the actual wound instead of being exactly over it. In this case, of course, the blood would spirt out readily enough. Besides, wounded tigers at once almost begin to lick off the blood flowing from any wound they can readily reach with their tongues. We constantly found the hair quite wet and turned back all round the bullet-holes. This they either do to relieve the pain, or to prevent their retreat being traced by the drops of blood they may lose at each step. In the evening we rode on to the village of "Beislah," four miles distant, where the tent had been sent.

We beat a large ravine two miles from this place, on the 21st, but it proved empty. After much questioning, the men admitted that there was another cover about three miles further on; so we at once walked across to the spot, but saw at a glance that the cover was too open to be at all likely to hold game. Moreover, some wood-cutters were still working there. Making still further inquiries at a few huts we passed on the road, we were told of a ravine near at hand in which a bear was said to reside, and that a tiger also had lately been seen there; so we hastened to beat this ravine, out of which we turned a bear. He got well "peppered," but the distance was too great to make sure of him. We tried another part of the cover, or a small branch of this large ravine, and put up a panther, at which we also fired and hit. After following up its prints and blood some little distance, we again saw the brute much hurt, and at once killed it outright. When we had taken off its skin it was nearly night-time, so we had a long walk over most rocky broken ground in the dark, and did not reach our tent till very late, well tired and hungry after such a long day's work.

A friend's gun we had borrowed to-day met with a sad accident. The man to whom it was entrusted slipped over a rock, and the barrels were cruelly dented in, rendering it quite unserviceable until afterwards repaired in camp.

Marched with our kit as far as "Buddana," eight miles, on the 22nd. Here we were told of some bullocks having lately been killed by tigers, so got together about a dozen men and went to a cover two miles off, and were directed to post ourselves on a bank overlooking the place. Soon a fine tiger turned out of a cave a little above where we had been so wrongly placed. We could not fire, for we caught but the merest glimpse of his hind quarters as he made off over a small hill. We gave chase, but without being able to again see him. It was too late, and the ground much too stony to attempt following up the prints.

Next day we again beat this same cover, first going very quietly to look at the cave out of which yesterday's tiger was started; but it was empty. The men turned out a tigress with two half-grown cubs, but the place was too thick for us to see clearly to fire, so we ran ahead in the hope of getting a shot at them in more open ground. But they were too cunning, for they left the cover and went over a small hill in the opposite direction to what we expected would be their course. We again went round a long way to try and drive them back. Here we suddenly met the two young tigers, but without their mother. Little attended to one while I took the other. Both were floored, but owing to the long grass we could not obtain a second shot at them. We followed up their blood for at least one mile and half, but could nowhere again discover these little brutes, although there was an unusual quantity of blood about. A heavy storm now caused us to desist, for the rain at once washed out all traces; so we returned to the tent, vexed to think that these young tigers would die without our getting their skins.

Once more we beat this cover and two others about a mile apart. Out of the last we started a young tiger and shot him. He managed to pass us, but was soon afterwards found dead in the long grass, on our following up his blood. Some monkeys now began making a great noise ahead, so we beat about a mile more of this cover, but without seeing any other tiger. Got home rather late, having about seven miles to walk back.

For the next six days, although we moved our camp daily, and hunted over some very likely-looking ground, we saw no big game. The men started a tiger out of one place, but we did not see it. We killed some sambur deer for the sake of the leather. By this time we had moved back to "Deypoora," hunting along the hills.

Here we suffered severely from the bees. Having failed to observe some nests of these insects in the clump of shady trees under which our camp was pitched, they were disturbed by the smoke of a fire our servants had made to cook by, and at once turned out by swarms, attacking every body and animal, especially our horses, that were picketed in a row close to our tent. These poor beasts began to kick and plunge fearfully, so, thinking to give them a chance of escape, I ran towards them and cut their head and heel ropes with my large hunting knife, getting well stung while so doing. But the horses being now free, instead of at once running away, as we had hoped they would do, began to fight with each other in the most fearful manner, being all, no doubt, perfectly maddened by the stings of the bees (myriads of which were flying about); they reared, bit, and kicked each other most desperately, till at last becoming entangled in the loose ropes by which they had been tethered, all five stallions were rolling on the ground together making a terrible noise and dust.

The bees now attacked me so badly that I was obliged to leave the horses and run for it, which I did, followed by a swarm of bees, until a stump tripped me up, when they punished me fearfully, although I had a soldier's great coat on at the time. One of our goats passed me crying piteously, with a swarm of bees about it. This poor goat died then and there from the stings, after going a few yards further. The greyhounds made off full speed across the open plain, loudly calling out, "Ping! ping! ping!" for each had its escort of bees at its tail. But at the time nobody was much inclined to laugh at their efforts to escape by flight, for every one of our men got dreadfully stung.

Little alone luckily escaped, having at the first alarm secured his blanket, in which he remained rolled up quite safe. We could not venture back to our tent till long after dark, when the bees had again become quiet. Everything was quickly removed far from such a dangerous neighbourhood. We next had to catch the horses. These poor animals were much swollen all over their bodies, for these wild bees are very large, and sting far worse than the common English bee. When one nest is disturbed, the other swarms in the neighbourhood seem to also turn out to their assistance. On a very large tree, not far from this spot, we counted eighteen bees' nests, each about two feet long by about fifteen inches broad. Up this tree were the marks of bears' claws distinctly visible, for bears are in the habit, at night, of climbing up after the honey, of which they are very fond. The Bheels declared they had seen one, by moonlight, seated along a branch, clawing down these nests with both paws, and greedily swallowing bees, wax, honey and all, seeming quite proof against their stings. It was very usual to find marks of where bears had climbed trees, on which were bees' nests, so this account seems likely enough to be true.

The bees had disabled me, robbed me of my sight for a time, and laid me on my back with fever. Little went out hunting alone.

CHAPTER XI.

WATER IN THE JUNGLE—TRACKS ROUND IT—UNWHOLESOME—FISH HARD UP FOR WATER—UNBORN CUBS—TIGER QUARRELS—GESTATION, AGE, HABITS—CAUTION AND FATAL WANT OF IT—END OF THE CAMPAIGN—THE "BAG."

IN his solitary chase my friend had seen a tiger, but had not been able to get a clear shot at him. Besides there was little water in the neighbourhood, and he thought that, if left undisturbed, this tiger would be likely to fall under our combined fire. When I recovered, however, we searched for him, but found him not. On the scarcity of water we placed great hopes of finding game. On inspecting a small pool of water, perhaps the only one for miles round, for the intense heat at this time of the year soon dries up the small streams, the hunter finds it easy to discover what kind of game might be expected to be met with in the surrounding jungle, as the different animals' footmarks would be clearly stamped in the mud round the water at which they come down to drink every night. The several small paths leading to this water were always most carefully examined by the men who hunted with us. From long practice they can tell to a certainty, by the appearance of a foot print, almost the number of hours since it was made. We also, in time, became quite expert at this business, for it was quite a pleasure to note by this means the presence of the various creatures in the immediate neighbourhood. Besides, some little dexterity was required to make out these marks, for as each different animal travelled in turn backwards and forwards to the water, they half obliterated each each other's steps, making it quite a puzzle to decipher them.

This will be easily understood when it is remembered, that over the same narrow path have walked perhaps a tiger, bear, panther, cheetah, hyæna, wolf, jackals, monkeys, foxes, porcupine, wild cats, sambur, "cheetul," gazelles, hog, "neelghaiee," &c., &c., with pea-fowl innumerable. The water was often very muddy, and even quite green and stagnant from decayed leaves and moss; yet many a time we were thankful enough to get a taste of it, even though one had to lie down and suck it up through a handkerchief four times doubled, to prevent the swallowing of particles of dead sticks, leaves, gnats' spawn. There were mostly plenty of wasps and bees round it, but on these occasions they never noticed us. Climbing over steep hills at this hot time of the year creates such intense thirst that any sort of water is welcome; but of course it must be very unwholesome. To drinking bad water we attributed the "guinea worms" with which our servants were so frequently afflicted in their feet, but we somehow managed to escape this painful plague.

By this time we had worked round again to "Rajghur" village, but were surprised to find the large piece of water here quite dry, except one small puddle which seemed literally alive with fish, as they wriggled in the muddy pool only a few yards round. We were amused at watching the numerous large kites and vultures, flocks of which were perched on all the high trees round about, as they dived down to this mass of fish, and actually carried them away, flying off with them in their claws and beaks. The smell from the quantities of dead fish round this "tank," or small lake, was so offensive that we were obliged to move our tent to a village two miles off. Numbers of small fresh-water turtle, with their shells smashed in, were scattered on the rocky shores of this dried up water. These, the men assured us, they had seen the kites pounce upon, and drop from a great height in the air, whereby the shell was cracked open, when the bird flew down to feed on the mangled remains of the tortoise; but we did not ourselves witness this feat, although, from the appearance of the small turtle-shells, it seemed highly probable.

On 6th June, we marched to "Naal," a village eight miles northwards. Here a Bheel stated that a tiger had lately killed several head of cattle, and readily offered to point out its den. We went very silently to the spot and threw in some stones, but the beast was declared to be "not at home." Just as we were about to leave the place, the tiger was seen quietly creeping off among some very thick thorn bushes, about thirty yards in our front, having turned out of another cave close by. We fired, and she instantly disappeared with loud roars in the dense jungle. We now began following up the tracks. This thicket was so full of tangled brushwood that we were compelled to crawl on our hands and knees; so we only took men enough to carry the spare guns. After going thus cautiously for about two hundred yards, which took some time, we came upon the tigress, quite dead, just at the end of the cover. On, as usual, opening her, to make the body lighter to carry, we were surprised to find that she would have given birth, in a day or two, to three young ones. These little things were completely formed, with the hair and stripes, teeth and claws, distinctly marked. They were about a foot long each, including their tails. There were two tigresses and a tiger, which seems to be the proportion of the sexes in these animals, for we met with quite double as many female as male tigers; but the Bheels declare that an old male tiger would certainly kill a young male if he caught him unawares at any time. This may perhaps, account for the disproportion.

Talking of their thus destroying each other, we were told by a Capt. M——, long a political officer in this country, that he was once long kept awake at night at the town of "Nundwass," a few miles from this place, by the terrible roaring of two large tigers. These brutes were fighting over the body of a bullock one of them had just killed, close to the walls of the small town. Next morning a tiger was found dead by the bullock's side, and on following up some tracks a short distance, the inhabitants found another tiger also dead. Both were large males, covered with marks from each other's claws and teeth. Like the Kilkenny cats, they had contrived to annihilate each other.

We could not discover for certain how long the tigress goes with young; the men here all agreed that it was only nine weeks, which seems a very short time for such a large animal; but as its living depends upon its activity, nature has perhaps kindly shortened the time that the tigress, big with young, may be prevented hunting for its food. The end of June, or commencement of the rains, seems to be the usual time of their breeding, when they retire to some dry cave and are extremely savage, roaring at any one who has chanced to approach within a long distance even of their den. Four cubs seem to be the greatest number, but they mostly have only two at a time.

We were unable to tell accurately the age of tigers, excepting by their size, discoloured appearance of the teeth, or faintness of the stripes. There was little else to judge by; the common idea that their age may be told by the number of lobes in the liver, (a fresh one for every year), seemed no criterion at all, for some perfect monsters had sometimes as few or less than the number found on evidently young tigers scarcely full grown. The "tusks" again, in many instances, were either solid ivory or quite hollow, without any regard to the size of the animals. Accounts, too, of their length of life also differed greatly, but twenty years seemed to be the common opinion as the tiger's greatest age. The cubs live with the mother till quite half grown. On several occasions we noticed that on beating a cover the young tigers invariably first made their appearance, as if they had been sent on by the mother to draw our fire.

So these little brutes were mostly allowed to pass by unhurt, when the old tigress was pretty sure to soon after follow in their wake. But, after all, this seemingly unnatural conduct of their parent may be explained by supposing that the cubs were more easily alarmed by the strange noise of the men, and led to escape, while the tigress, more cunning, merely waited to see whether the coast was clear before leaving her stronghold.

In many cool, shady places, where a tigress and her family had been lying during the heat of the day, we used to find the high green reeds or dry grass trampled down all round, evidently the work of the cubs, while playing with one another. The mother, too, had perhaps joined in these gambols. This, coupled with the extraordinary beauty of the surrounding scenery, which we could not help remarking in many instances, where these animals had chosen their retreats, gave rise to the idea that, in spite of the very general opinion to the contrary, perhaps, after all, in private life, "the tiger" may have a soul as full of poetry as the "Coavinses" in "Bleak House."

Beat a small cover near the village on June 7th, but it was empty. Soon after we heard pea-fowl and sambur calling on a hill close by, which proved that some wild animal was disturbing them. This hill was so covered with dense brushwood, that game could only be seen a few yards off. We stood sentry over a narrow path, while the men went round to beat, and presently a fine panther made his appearance. After looking at us for a few seconds, he turned off without our being able to get a clear shot at him, owing to the density of the jungle. An old bear next came shuffling along the path, but not being so cautious as the panther, he came close by where we were posted, when we fired into him, whereon he rushed screaming and groaning terribly down the steep side of the hill. We soon saw him slowly climbing a hill directly opposite, so we at once gave chase, and soon added him to our bag.

Ordered off the kit to "Oomurtunah," a village seven miles

distant, and again went to look for yesterday's panther, but could not find him. Tried some patches of jungle near our halting-place for a tiger that had lately killed a buffalo there, but without success; and were obliged to leave off hunting, on account of a sudden shower of rain, that completely drenched us all.

On the next day we moved on to "Paat" village, but only caught a glimpse of him as he quickly bolted out among some very thick brushwood.

On the 10th June, we again looked for this last seen tiger, but could not meet him anywhere; and so we sent on the camels to "Beejeepoor," but heavy rain spoilt all hope of finding game, although we beat some likely covers. The tent even was soaked wet through.

On the 11th, we went to look at some hills near this town covered with thick thorn-bushes. The men soon put out a very fine panther. It came slowly on towards our position, and seemed so large, stout, and light coloured, that at the distance we mistook it for a tigress. We both fired together, and rolled the beast over, but it instantly regained its legs, and came charging down in magnificent style, roaring and bounding over the high bushes at a lightning pace. More shots were fired, when we all at once lost sight of the panther, nor could we again discover him, although we followed his tracks, of which there was plenty, a long way, until another heavy fall of rain stopped the pursuit, by washing out the traces. We then rode on to "Panghur," our original starting point of this year's shooting expedition, where the tent had been sent six miles distant.

We were now approaching the end of our campaign. The rain began to fall in frequent showers, spoiling sport. While in the "Bahara" ravine, we heard a cuckoo call most distinctly this morning, and saw the bird, the first of the sort either of us had yet met with in India.

A perfect hurricane raged on the night of the 14th. There were actually small waves on the large tank or lake there; and in the morning we found all our gun-barrels brimfull of water, they having been piled against the walls of the tent. We had much trouble in cleaning so many guns before we could take a farewell look for the panther there. We visited all his most likely haunts, but without being able to discover the beast, and then returned to our tent and busily assisted to pack up our baggage for its last march to Camp Neemuch, our leave having expired that day. We first emptied our pouches of the usual quantity of ammunition, that we each carried thirty rounds, by smashing a few beer bottles placed at long distances as marks, which bottles we had previously emptied at a mild "tiffin," or lunch, under the trees, while our camels were being loaded. We both agreed that we had passed as pleasant a time of it in these woods as any we had spent in India. Then we mounted our fresh Arab horses, and reached camp by dusk, well pleased at the result of our sporting trip.

The following head of large game were brought to bag in this year's shooting excursion. Twenty-four tigers killed, ten tigers wounded, or perhaps eleven. Two panthers killed, two panthers wounded. Nine bears killed, four bears wounded, besides several deer of different sorts killed and wounded. Total "large game" killed and wounded, fifty-one.

CHAPTER XII.

Third campaign, 1852—Joined by a new comrade—Serious and exciting incident—Escape of Mr. Elliot—Join a strong party—Escape of Dr. M——Left alone—Wet weather and no sport—Bruin plentiful—Habits of bears.

In the spring of 1852, I once more obtained leave of absence for three months, and returned for the third time to the jungle. I departed from camp on the 16th March, and spent two days fruitlessly seeking game in the covers near "Panghur," and the ravine at "Bahara." When I returned to my tent on the evening of the 18th, I was delighted to meet Cornet Elliot, of the 1st Bombay Lancers, who had that day ridden out from camp to join me in this year's shooting expedition.

We set to work at once, and on the 19th walked four miles across country to some steep rocks called "Palsee," at which place bullocks were reported to have been lately killed by tigers, but after beating all the likely covers about, we saw nothing but an old hyæna, at which of course we did not fire. Our next move was to "Dowlutpoora," a village six miles off; but owing to the bad rocky road and heavy rain that fell at night, our kit did not reach us till next morning. That night we slept under a tree, getting rather damp by the rain. Again beat the "Bahara" cover near this village, but could not discover the tiger said to live here, although our hopes were excited by hearing the peacocks call. Only a wild cat was turned out after all. There being no other likely places for game near, we at once rode on to "Rajghur," twelve miles, getting wet through on the road by the heavy rain that again fell; our guns and baggage did not arrive till midnight.

The morning of the 21st March was passed in cleaning our guns, that had become rusty from yesterday's rain; but by noon, having assembled thirty-eight Bheels, we set out to beat a ravine two miles off. This place proved blank, so we walked across to another cover, called "Bunda," three miles distant. This did not appear at all a likely-looking piece of ground to hold tigers; however, we agreed to beat it, expecting merely to perhaps find sambur. Here we had a serious adventure.

To enable us to overlook the high grass around, we both got up a small thorn-tree with our guns. Scarcely had the beaters commenced making their usual noise, when a fine tiger appeared, to our great delight, slowly walking straight towards us. We silently agreed to let it come on within a few yards of our post before firing, when, much to our annoyance, a man who had climbed up a high tree a little distance beyond our position called out most unnecessarily to warn us of the tiger's approach, thinking we had not observed it. This noise at once caused the tiger to stop and stare round for a moment, when it bounded off at a good pace in an opposite direction. We instantly fired our double rifles and one gun-barrel at the brute, and well knew our shots had told by its loud growls; but it was out of sight in the thick jungle around before we could obtain other shots. Those we did fire were very uncertain and hurried, and at a much greater distance than would have been the case had not this tiger been so unluckily disturbed from its course towards our tree. We waited to allow the men to finish beating the cover, and soon heard some pea-fowl calling. Directly afterwards a small tiger made its appearance, and was rolled over with a single ball; but on the Bheels coming up, we could nowhere find this cub, for it had managed to crawl off unseen and hide itself in the long grass, where it was found dead two days after.

We did not like to waste our time looking for it long, as the evening was coming on, so at once began following up the prints and blood of the big wounded tiger. These we took, with some little difficulty, through a dense patch of thorn-bushes and high grass, for about three hundred yards, keeping all the men well together in a body while we led the way. Presently we came out of this thick jungle on an open space, but here all traces of the tiger suddenly ceased. Placing a man from time to time up the low trees we passed, to look out all round, Elliot and myself advanced a few paces in front of the men, to more minutely examine the ground for the tracks, before they should be obliterated or trampled over by the feet of so many persons following us. While thus engaged in carefully endeavouring to recover the lost tracks of this wounded tiger, we were startled by a loud roar from a small ditch a few paces on our right. At this time Elliot was stooping down about twenty yards on my left, busily employed in looking for prints. The roar was instantly followed by the tiger, that came charging down at great speed straight for me. I had barely time to fire both barrels of my rifle, at only two or three paces' distance, into her chest, when these shots, or the smoke, caused the beast to swerve past me and make straight for Elliot, whom she at once sprang on, literally before he had time to get his rifle ready. The next moment I saw him falling backwards under the tigress, which was growling and roaring over him fearfully. My "shikarrees," with admirable coolness and presence of mind, quickly handed me spare loaded guns. I instantly fired two more shots at the beast's shoulder, as she stood over poor Elliot, but these wounds had little effect, for she at once commenced dragging him backwards, by the upper part of his left arm, which she had seized in her jaws, down a gentle slope, towards the ditch in which she had at first been lying hid. The ground was very uneven, and covered with broken pieces of rock, so I greatly feared to again fire at this

Lieut W. Rice, Del. M & N Hanhart, lith

ELLIOT BEING SEIZED

tigress lest my friend should be hit instead; for as his face was touching her head, no steady shot could be had at her brain, as she bumped him over these rough stones. Elliot had fainted while the tigress was thus carrying him off. She continued growling all the time, and looked full at us as the rest of the men and I followed at about eight paces' distance, watching to get a clear shot at her head (for it would have been useless to have fired at any other part.) At last, after aiming two or three times in vain, there was a chance, when my ball luckily struck her on the top of the skull, whereupon she at once dropped poor Elliot, and rolled over dead on the top of his body, bringing her paw down on his chest. I quickly gave her the other barrel, and then ran in with the rest of the Bheels, and pulled out Elliot by his legs from under the tigress.

While she was thus walking him off, the men were greatly excited. On the tigress first charging there was, as usual, a general move backwards for a step, whereby many were upset; but they immediately followed in a body, and much wished me to let them bravely attack the tigress with what arms they had, such as swords, spears, iron-pointed clubs, axes, and bows—especially Elliot's own servant, who, with the best intentions of frightening off the tigress, discharged several guns in the air, regardless of direction, firing them from his hip in the most alarming manner, and loudly protesting that his master was killed; which really did seem likely enough, for he was covered with blood.

On our lifting him up, Elliot was quite sensible, and asked for water. He was quickly supplied with a long drink from the "chagul," or leathern bag to hold water, which we invariably carried with us out hunting. His arm, which was frightfully bitten, was at once bound up in a long turban, while the men busied themselves in cutting down small trees, from which, with the help of a general contribution of turbans, waist-cloths, and slight green boughs, we formed a sort of litter, and then started for "Rajghur," about two and a half miles distant, through the jungle, followed by the rest of the men carrying the dead tigress, which was a very stout fine beast.

Elliot, on being first seized, had a narrow escape from a blow she had aimed at him with her paw, which he fortunately guarded off with his uplifted rifle. The stock of the rifle was marked with her claws, while the triggers and guard were knocked completely flat on one side, so that the gun was useless until repaired. The tigress only dragged him about twenty or thirty yards, and the whole "scrimmage" was over in two or three minutes. From lying hid so close in the deep ditch, which was covered with long grass, the man placed on the look-out up the tree had failed to observe her, which he must have done had the ground been level. While following up this wounded tigress we several times observed a "kole balloo," or old jackal, that trotted on a few score paces in our front.

On reaching our tent at "Rajghur," my servant was at once started on a pony for camp, about thirty-two miles off, with orders to ride as fast as he could, so that a "doolee" (a sort of palanquin or litter, for the use of the sick or wounded of an army) might be sent out to help bring home poor Elliot, who was now in great pain. While we set out directly for "Jaat," the nearest town where there was any chance of getting fresh men to carry the cot on which Elliot was now borne on the shoulders of about a dozen Bheels. The road was very hilly and uneven, passing over broken stony ground, and we could only go at a slow pace. The night, too, was very dark, with much rain, so that after travelling all night long, we were still sixteen miles from camp when daylight broke, having been delayed a good deal with getting relays of bearers, guides, and torches, at the different villages on our road. About seven miles from camp we met the "doolee," when I wished Elliot good by, to return to my sport, as I could no longer be of any use to him.

Hearing that a party of officers were encamped at "Suckdeo," a beautiful place for a picnic party, about fifteen miles from camp, I rode to meet them, and was glad enough to get there, being very hungry and tired. After breakfast, or tiffin rather, we went to beat the hills here in company with the chief of "Athana" who had collected a number of men for the purpose. Nothing was turned out but a wretched hyæna that was quickly murdered, not for sport but merely for want of something to unload the guns at. More rain fell at night; and in the morning some Bheels came in, saying they had seen fresh prints of a tiger leading towards a large ravine about half a mile from the tents.

Colonel D——, Drs. C—— and M——, and myself, set out to look for the beast. We could only muster three double guns and my pistols among the party. On reaching the ravine, having decided how it was to be beaten, Dr. C—— took up one position at the entrance of the cover which he guarded with his gun, while Colonel D—— and myself, with one gun each, climbed a tree in the middle of the ravine a little higher up. Dr. M——, who had merely joined the party as a spectator, got up a low tree a few yards on our left, leaving one of my double pistols, with which weapon alone he had taken the field, at the foot of his tree. The remaining double pistol was entrusted to the beaters, with directions for them to fire blank shots while driving this cover. Almost directly after the noise of the beaters was heard at the far end of this steep ravine, a splendid tiger was seen coming straight towards us at a quick pace along the bed of a dry watercourse or "nullah." We allowed him to come close up before firing our four shots, which rolled him over; but very soon after he recovered his legs and began staring about him, seemingly much confused which course to take. Before we had time to reload, the tiger moved a few steps slowly up a bank on the right. Here he caught sight of Dr. M——, who was dressed in white clothes, and stood perfectly motionless on a low bough of a small tree, about twenty paces from the tiger. After taking a long earnest stare at Dr. M——, who had the presence of mind not to move, the beast quietly walked into a very thick patch of "corinda" bushes close by, and was no more seen by us, although we tried for some time longer to dislodge him by rolling down large rocks, &c., from above, until a sudden heavy shower of rain put a stop to all further attempts for that day.

Dr. C—— was too far off to get a shot at this tiger. Dr. M——'s position was by no means an enviable one, for he was perfectly unarmed, and the tiger by a spring could easily have pulled him out of the tree. But on my mentioning this story to my "shikarrees," they assured me that the tiger no doubt mistook Dr. M——, from the fact of his keeping so perfectly still, for a mere white piece of cloth, or some such object, with which native chiefs are in the habit of scaring any animal from passing by any particular part of the jungle in which they are hunting, by hanging up on the bushes around some such conspicuous marks.

Early next day the rest of our party were obliged to return to camp, but I borrowed their guns for a few hours, and again set out to look for this wounded tiger, taking twelve Bheels with me. We carefully looked through the whole of this beautiful cover, in the hopes of finding the brute either dead or dying, but the heavy rain that fell overnight had quite washed out his prints. At length we found some hair on some broken twigs of a bush at the entrance of this ravine, which proved the tiger had left this cover during the night. He was found dead two days after by some people collecting "korinda" berries, not above three hundred yards from this very spot, but of this fact at the time we had nothing to guide us. I returned to the tents to breakfast, but was vexed to find the pony on which I had ridden here so lame, that it was obliged to be sent into camp, so there was the treat in store for me of walking across a very stony country a good twelve miles to "Jaat," where I had ordered my servant, on his return from camp with the "doolee," to await my arrival. Taking a guide, who carried my saddle and bridle on his head, I reached Jaat by half past four P. M., then rode my own pony back to "Rajghur," which place I reached after dark.

Wet weather continued for the next fortnight, during which time rain fell daily more or less; moreover, the weather, for the time of year, was quite cool; terrible drawbacks these for all chance of sport; for, where there is so much water about (even pools of it lying on the tops of the highest hills), the "large game" has, of course, no need to resort to particular spots to drink; or, in such cool weather, to seek the shadiest covers, for protection from the intense heat. Any small bush, then, serves for a tiger or bear to lie up in during the day. Besides, as they no longer had cause to fear burning their feet by travelling over hot rocky ground, the slightest noise was sufficient to cause them to move off at once in any direction, long before the hunter could hit upon their hiding place, however silently or cautiously he might go to work.

For the next six days, although I hunted from morning to night, no large game was to be seen in any of the likely covers I tried, except an old bear, at which I got a long shot as he was going over a steep hill. This brought the bear rolling and screaming down the hill-side almost to my feet, but he was lost in some very high thick grass or reeds at the bottom of this hill, in spite too of plenty of blood we found, but could not trace far; but better luck was at hand.

On the 1st April, while silently going ahead with two

men carrying my spare guns to take up a position previous to beating the "Kell" ravine at "Doraee" village, we suddenly came upon two large bears feeding under a "moura" tree on the ripe berries that had fallen below. I divided equally my six barrels on the pair of brutes as fast as possible, whereupon they began fighting with each other in the most laughable style, for some few minutes making a fearful noise, when they separated, and each bolted off into some high grass close at hand before I had reloaded even one gun. There was plenty of blood about; but, while following up these bears, we suddenly found quite fresh prints of a very large tiger, so I regretted having fired at the bears, and at once discontinued looking for them. On trying another branch of this ravine, the men started a bear, which I did not see; but, on going to yet another cover still further on, towards which we had tracked the tiger, another bear came so close by me that it was impossible to resist firing. I gave him two shots, when he made off moaning pitcously. Monkeys began to swear, and peacocks to call, directly after my firing these last shots, so, no doubt, this bear caused me to lose the tiger, that must have moved off unseen at the noise of my gun. I did not think of again firing at the bear on hearing the monkeys. Four bears in the space of about a mile square was good allowance. They were no doubt attracted to this place by the quantity of "moura" trees about, which at this season were in full blossom. The flower smells very sweet, and can be scented from a long distance; the fruit, or berries, are also ripe at this same time of year.

On a former occasion when hunting in the province of "Candeish" with a friend, we found several bears collected in this manner in a small compass, they having been attracted by the soft sweet root of a particular sort of pine-tree. We managed to kill eight, besides wounding three other bears that escaped us, in the space of four days. Bears, after all, are not so easily killed as from this might be supposed. They often require an astonishing amount of lead to finish them, and the hunter has to take care of himself besides. Many a time have I had to make the best use of my legs to avoid a charging bear. The sport, of course, is not to be compared with panther or tiger shooting in point of danger. Still there is plenty of excitement in it, and it affords the very best practice to enter a beginner at "large game" hunting. Accidents at this sport are common enough, but seldom fatal to the hunter. The natives have a very proper dread of bears, for many a poor woodcutter, having nothing but his small axe to defend himself with, has been killed by these beasts. At almost every village in this country near the hills a man can be found who carries the scars on his body of wounds received from bears, generally from his having accidentally wandered near the den of a she bear with cubs, at which time they are very savage, and will charge any one, whether hunting them or not. Bears' meat is coarse but good eating, for they feed entirely on roots, fruit, honey, and never touch flesh unless the nests of white ants and large sort of slugs can be so considered. He digs up the nests, and overthrows large stones to find grubs and worms.

CHAPTER XIII.

Fruitless toil—Hunting "cheetah"—A long shot and a charge—A lost prize—A jungle on fire—A shot in the water—Dangerous work—The game escapes—Ill luck continues—An exciting chase—Snakes—Too much cover—A tiger's leap—Robbing the bees—A shot through the liver.

Even in the prolific jungle large game does not everywhere abound. For the next seven days I sought diligently, but found nothing, except, when returning one evening wearied, an old bear which I wounded, but which, after all, escaped me.

The tent had been moved on, almost daily, a few miles along the hills towards "Kooakhera" village, to enable me to hunt over fresh ground each day, but no tiger could we see; although, on one occasion, while following up some fresh prints of one in a dry river bed, we constantly heard a "kole balloo," or old jackal, calling just in front of us. Twice my men stopped short, and pointed silently to what, at the time, we all thought must be the tiger lying up under some thick bushes; but we were mistaken, though only a few yards off, for these turned out to be nothing but large red rocky stones. It is very difficult sometimes to make out a tiger when thus concealed in grass or bushes, for they will often lie very close, and their skin of the same colour as the dry grass and reeds around, while the stripes even, if seen, are easily mistaken for shadows cast by the strong glare of the sun. It luckily happened for me that we were this time mistaken, for, on going home to my tent, I aimed at a very large alligator basking asleep on a bank by the river side, but both my caps missed fire, having become damp from the continued wet weather. To prevent accidents of this sort occurring, we made it a rule to always change the gun caps for fresh ones every morning. One day, soon after this, while thus tracking a tiger, as silently as possible, we found that the brute must have been moving off a long way just in front of us, for we came upon his fresh prints over the marks made by a flock of goats that had been driven along a road only a few minutes before. This proves how easily the "large game" moves about, even in the day time, during such cool weather. On still further following this tiger's tracks, we came upon a dead hunting "cheetah" (or hunting leopard) that had just been killed by the tiger, he having, no doubt, surprised the "cheetah" asleep, for the marks of the tiger's claws, from which blood still was flowing, were quite plain on the body.

This animal (harmless enough except for deer) he must have killed in mere wantonness. On another occasion we found a hyæna that had been thus murdered by a tiger, perhaps for heedlessly passing too close to him. The paw alone had been used to kill these victims, for there were no teeth marks. It struck me as rather odd to find a "hunting cheetah" in the hills, for these animals live mostly in the plains, where they hunt deer or antelope in parties of four or five together, in the same manner as the wolves do, secreting themselves in bushes at different points while one of their number chases the buck. On its passing the ambuscade they pounce out upon the little gazelle, or take up the running in turn as it races past them.

On the 9th April, I set out to beat the upper end of the "Booj" river, and seeing how quickly the game moved off at the least noise during this cool weather, determined to have a very long drive indeed. We went a mile, at least, ahead of the beaters. Presently I saw a very fine tiger coming slowly on, but as he seemed inclined to turn up a small branch of this big ravine, I was obliged to fire, though at 120 yards' distance. This shot luckily broke his fore arm, whereupon he came roaring down towards me as fast as his disabled leg would allow. This gave me time for four more shots, the last of which rolled him over much crippled, for he halted in some very thick patch of willow bushes about thirty yards off, where I could hear him growling terribly, but could not see him at all. After waiting for the men to come up, we threw volleys of stones into this thick patch of jungle, but could not turn out the tiger. I fired on guess nearly forty other shots into this place, when suddenly the tiger was quiet. Then, very cautiously, we approached the place in a body, and, luckily, found the tiger dead. His body was much protected from my shots by two large rocks between which he was lying, but a chance bullet had struck his head, and settled him. We skinned him on the spot, which job was not finished till dusk, so we did not get back to the tent till late, having six miles to walk. I pegged the skin down by candlelight, fearing it might shrink—it measured eleven feet eight inches long, and was very wide.

For the next five days, as the weather still continued so cool, I did not get a shot at any "large game." At one cover a bear passed by me, but expecting to find a tiger there, I did not fire at him. At "Ambah," a cattle-owner had lately poisoned two or three tigers by placing arsenic in the bodies of the bullocks the tigers had killed. This accounted for my finding no sport in any of the good covers about there.

By 15th April, my tent having been sent on to "Bhynsrode Fort," I went across the river "Chumbul" to "Amtee Amlee" village, where the people told me that a tiger had that day killed a bullock. Having collected some Bheels, we went to his usual dwelling place. I was posted up a small tree to overlook the long grass and thick bushes, when, soon after the beaters had commenced their work, a fine tiger appeared. He had nearly escaped me unseen, owing to the thick cover; but as he was just going over a high bank on my left, I viewed him in time to hastily fire one shot at his shoulders. This brought him bounding down the steep bank in two long springs, close under the low tree in which I was stuck up. Here he got another bullet, but was out of sight in the long grass beyond before another gun could be got ready. Thinking he might be rolled over for good, as there was a great quantity of blood about, I waited for the Bheels to come up, when we began following up the blood in a compact body. Presently we heard some low growls about forty yards ahead, but could see nothing, for the grass here was very thick and at least nine feet high. We now stopped, but the growling noise still continued. This tiger clearly had more life in him than we expected, so we slowly retreated, showing a front, however, for we half expected to be charged every minute. There was no tree near on this open plain, and we had therefore no means of finding out the exact spot where he was lying hid. The men did not wish the grass to be burnt, as they intended cutting it for their cattle; besides had we done so no one could have gone near such a fire, which would be likely to burn for days, driving every head of game clean out of the country as it extended over the surrounding jungle. I was forced to let this tiger alone, and ride on reluctantly to my tent at "Bhynsrode." His prints, on hard ground, measured six inches long by five wide, so he was a monster. I saw a very large lynx, at least two feet high and very long, but could not fire. He came close by me without being aware of my presence, and was the largest animal of the kind I had yet met with in these parts.

On 17th April, went, with about twenty men, to beat "Paradur" ravine. The Bheels there saw an old bear lying outside his cave, but on their approach he retreated to his den. We could not drive him out, being afraid to apply lighted grass or sticks for fear of disturbing the bees, whose nests were very numerous on all the high rocks around. On beating the cover shortly afterwards, a fine tiger came by my post; I dropped him with a single ball in the head, but was obliged to give him three more shots for trying to get up again a little while after he had fallen, having been only stunned at first. These shots killed him outright. He measured eleven feet nine inches long. Being near the place, I much wished to have a look for the tiger wounded two days ago, but skinning this last killed one made it too late, as we had a long walk home.

The jungle all round here had been set on fire. This is done every year to cause fresh green blades of grass to spring up for the cattle to eat. But it spoils all chance of sport in the neighbourhood. At night the red line of fire of the burning grass looks very pretty as it appears in waving red lines over the distant hills. The jungle, when thus burnt, will continue on fire for days together; columns of black smoke by day pointing out the course of the fire; while at night there seems to be a general illumination in the woods. The heat is very great from this burning grass. I have sometimes, on meeting it, had to run quickly through the long thin line of fire, taking good care to first throw my powder horn over on the other side a long way. A person might walk for a mile or more before finding an opening in this wall of flames.

From "Bhynsrode" I moved on by easy stages to "Mundulghur," but without finding any tigers, for the country was very open. While bathing in a piece of water near which my tent was pitched, rather late in the evening, one of my servants came to say that a bear had come down to drink on the opposite shore. I sent for the rifle, and walked after him in the water, until within about thirty yards. The shots told well, for with loud groans he bolted back into the jungle. It was too dark to look for him then, and by next morning he had managed to walk off. There were a good many sambur about in this part of the country, but I did not fire at them.

On the 22nd of April, after a long march with my camels across an open cultivated country—for I was anxious to get back to better ground—we arrived at a village where a man was reported to have been lately killed by a tiger in a very large ravine named "Noorsinghur." Having sent round to the different villages about for men, sixty-five of whom readily offered to help hunt for this tiger, I set out for the cover, which was far too wide to give me much chance of being able to guard even half of it. Choosing the narrowest part, I waited for the noise of the beaters to begin. Almost directly afterwards double pistol-shots, fired in rapid succession, gave me notice that the men had seen the tiger—for this was a signal agreed upon between us whenever a tiger or panther was known to be on foot, so that we might look out and not spoil sport by firing at only a bear or even "sambur." He was seen by the men placed above on either side of this big ravine on the look-out, to be slowly creeping along just in front of the beaters, who had brought him on from a long distance in beautiful style towards my post, which was on the top of a large rock, where I was lying down with my "battery" by my side, expecting every moment to see the tiger. Suddenly a tremendous roaring was heard in the midst, it seemed to me, of the beaters; they, too, set up extra shouts and noise, rapidly firing six blank shots from the pistols with which they were provided. Then all was still. I made quite sure that some poor fellow had been hurt, perhaps killed, and waited in the greatest state of suspense while the men came silently up to my rock, having left off the noise of beating.

It appeared that two men had foolishly left the body of Bheels and gone down to a stream in the middle of the cover to drink. The tiger at once saw them, and was observed by the men on the look-out above to crawl quietly towards these two fellows as if stalking them. They were quickly warned of their danger just in time, for they both jumped down into the water, as the tiger, with awful roars, rushed towards them on the bank where they had just been standing. Being disappointed of his prey, he broke back over the very ground he had been so unwillingly driven, roaring terribly as he ran off, to show his disgust at being so disturbed in the heat of the day. The men started to beat in two parties, keeping parallel with each other, and then joining when the cover got more narrow. Thus, through the stupidity of these two men, I lost an almost certain chance of killing this tiger, while they had a most wonderful escape from death. The foot-prints were enormous, and we found he had the night before killed a large buffalo. It was too late to again look for this tiger.

Next day I again tried with the same men to find this tiger; first going to a cover a little way off, where it was thought likely he had gone; but here the confounded bees turned out, so we had to leave the place at once, some men getting slightly stung.

Walking across to the big ravine we came upon the tiger's fresh prints; there was no mistaking their great size: besides, the brute was well known, and had been several times shot at by matchlock men, but with no effect. The beaters described this tiger as being very bold and fierce, killing buffaloes in broad daylight, close to the walls of their villages. We followed the tracks silently for nearly four miles, when finding he had left this part of the country altogether, I sent back word for my tent to be brought on to "Sawunt" village, six miles off, while I continued following up the prints till dark: a pursuit that compelled me to sleep out under a tree without any food, till next morning, for the road was so bad and stony that the camels could not get on at all. Besides, the men left behind to assist in getting them up the "ghaut," or steep hill, took themselves off without warning. A few smashes among my baggage was the consequence of these bad roads or mere paths rather. Rain unfortunately fell, too, during the night, so we could not carry on yesterday's prints any farther. The villagers had lately found a dead tiger here by some water; most likely it had been poisoned—a dirty trick, and the ruin of all sport; but they of course cannot view the matter in that light.

While looking over the ground here, on the 24th of April, I saw an old bear lying asleep at the mouth of a large cave, at least two hundred yards off, across a deep ravine. Fired three shots at her as she bolted down hill, on being woke up by my first bullet. Afterwards went round and saw plenty of blood, but did not attempt to follow up this bear. She bolted, growling, and was accompanied by a half-grown cub, that also came out of the cave.

The weather still continued much too cool for sport, for though every likely cover was tried, at the different places the tent was moved on to, yet nothing was seen worth firing at.

After putting up a great many sambur at Gole Ambah, on the 28th, I was tempted to fire at one for the men to eat. Directly the shot was fired, a bear turned out of a cave at my feet, a few yards only below. He quickly got the other barrel, which made him roar; but he rolled so fast down the steep rocks that formed the hill side, that I could not get another shot at him before he disappeared in some very dense jungle in the plain below.

Merely a few sambur were shot until the 2nd May, when I had marched on as far as "Buddana" village. While beating a cover there, a tiger was seen slowly going over a stony open hill, about 500 yards off. The ground being quite cool this mild weather, I at once ran round sharp on the other side as fast as possible, telling the men to begin beating towards me in a few minutes' time. Just as I had got round the hill the tiger came slowly on, about sixty yards off, when it saw me, and stopped still to take a good stare before passing on. This gave me a capital shot, which, to my delight, at once dropped the tiger, seemingly dead, for I had aimed at its head. The beaters shortly afterwards came up, and we were walking together towards the tiger, when, at about only twenty paces off, up the beast got, greatly to our surprise. Most of the men quickly sprang up trees, while I fired two more shots, as sharp as possible, at this tiger. On forming a procession to follow up the blood, we soon came upon it dead. My first bullet had struck exactly between the brute's eyes, a little too low, so it was only stunned. I did not fire other shots at the time, as some of the Bheels declared there were two tigers known to live in this cover, so hoped to see the other, but only this one appeared, which was a young tigress, a few inches over nine feet long, very prettily marked.

In consequence of the heavy showers, I had all the guns to clean on the 4th May. A ravine named "Ahmedghur," where there is a ruined large fort, about four miles off, was said to be a likely place, so I went there with twenty-five men. On the road we saw two large snakes, called "damuns," at least ten feet long; shot them both. These reptiles have the most wonderful power of holding on by twisting the end of their tails round any substance presented to them. When half dead, the men, for fun, placed a stout stick on the extreme end of their tails, which was immediately seized, and held so firmly, that it was released with the greatest difficulty. In this manner the Bheels assured me these snakes caught and destroyed hares, young goats, &c., but they did not think they were poisonous. Their colour was light brown, with a green tint above, and bright yellow bellies. The species does not seem common, for these were the first of the sort I had met.

On arriving at "Ahmedghur," we heard a troop of monkeys swearing on the top of high trees around, which told us what to expect. This ravine was so large that I was puzzled how to beat it, or where to post myself, and was unluckily persuaded to remain above on a precipice overlooking the cover. Almost immediately after the noise of the beaters began, out sprang a large tiger, but at least 120 yards off. I fired as he bounded down the steep hill side; the first shot missed, but my second bullet dropped him. He got up and crept into a small patch of very thick jungle just below me. There he remained for a long time, in spite of many shots fired at random into the thicket. At last I caught a glimpse of him, slowly moving on to another patch of high grass and "corinda" bushes, and made him roar loudly with another bullet; but this last retreat was even more dense than the first. After in vain trying to again make him show himself by firing away nearly all my ammunition at hazard into every corner of the cover, we went down in a body together to the first thicket. Here plenty of hair in tufts was found on the large rough stones over which he had dragged himself. The men bravely enough much wished me to follow him into the other dense mass of bushes and high reeds where he had retreated, but this I feared to do, for there was not room even to use a gun if we had come upon him, and there would very probably have been an accident. We were thus obliged to leave him alone. There were no trees about from which a view could be obtained over the cover. This is one of those cases in which elephants are absolutely necessary to find a wounded tiger, for no one could have seen even one yard ahead in such thick jungle. The tiger-hunter on foot thus loses many a fine skin that would be secured easily enough if an elephant trained to the sport were at hand. Still, in the absence of elephants, it is better to thus prudently lose a tiger occasionally than to forego the sport altogether for want of them. It was very annoying to have to refuse accompanying the Bheels to look for a wounded beast in such dense bushes. If allowed, they would willingly have gone alone, having exaggerated notions of the effect of our bullets from seeing other tigers killed. Directly a drop of blood even was found, the wounded brute was sure to be pronounced dead, when perhaps it was only rendered more lively and vicious from the wound. Such caution on the part of the hunter then is sure to be considered merely another name for fear, which in fact it is.

Next day I again went over to this ravine, but beat it first before looking for yesterday's tiger. Most unfortunately I took up another position below, for a tigress, quickly followed by her half grown cub, at once turned out, and, as ill luck would have it, sprang up the steep sides of the precipice over which I had yesterday kept guard. I fired two shots, but no doubt missed both, as the distance was over a hundred yards. These tigers, in two leaps, managed to reach the top of the rocky level above the ravine, though the sides were as straight as a wall, at least twenty-five feet high. They rested, for a moment only, on a small ledge about half way up, and then bounded over. None of the men, or myself, had the slightest idea that they could so escape; but the schemes of these cunning animals seem endless. I never yet saw any two act alike. Hence, there is much to learn at this sport. We next tried for the wounded tiger, and took his prints for some distance, until they ceased on very stony ground. He had, therefore, far more life in him than we supposed. The ravine here requires at least three guns posted in different points to guard it, being so wide and steep.

Our next operations were in a beautiful cover named "Earday," but we found no large game; a fact accounted for by our meeting a party of men who were taking honey, of which there was a great quantity, for the sides of the rocks that formed this ravine were covered with bees' nests. One or two Bheels, well protected with woollen clothes or coarse blankets, held up a pan of burning sulphur on the top of long bamboos, close to the bees' nests; and afterwards knocked down the combs with the poles. They had several large earthen pots full of honey, and did not seem to mind the bees at all, although we gladly made our escape from the spot. Going homewards, the men put two tigers out of a cover which we beat. These brutes at once left the place, and broke sideways over a steep bare hill, for it was raining at the time, and quite cool. Had the weather only been hotter, they would have remained in the shade, and no doubt have given me a fair shot as they passed by my post. For the next two days I saw no game, although we tried some very likely places a few miles further on. At one the men did not seem to like the work, for, while hunting with a chief here lately for sambur only, they were charged by a tigress with two young cubs, but no harm beyond the fright was done.

On the 9th May, I sent on my baggage to "Kunjaira" village, and went to beat "Bhogla" ravine, a fine cover, full of high willow-trees. After a long drive a fine tiger walked slowly out of the cover, and coolly sat down under a shady tree, about a hundred yards on one side, quite in an open space. Although the beaters were not far off, she did not seem to mind them at all. I was by a large tree about eighty yards off across the cover. I fired one shot as she was lying down. With a roar she jumped up, and galloped across a rather open space for some high grass a short distance beyond. My second barrel missed. On going up to the spot with the beaters, my bullet was found about an inch deep in the stump of the tree. Of course we all thought it had missed, but, on cutting it carefully out with an axe, one or two men seemed to think it was too clean and bright. We began following up the tiger's prints, and, after going about three hundred yards, suddenly came upon this tiger, quite dead, in the high grass. There was not a single drop of blood to be found anywhere about. The ball had passed clean through her liver. This was a fine tigress, nine feet four inches long, and very stout.

While following up this brute, most of the men seemed convinced she was hit in spite of there being no blood about, from the fact that, for a long distance, the ground was marked with her claws at each spring or leap she had made while bounding away. This, they declared, would not be the case if the beast was not wounded, for the action was very unnatural, and only caused by great rage and pain. A tiger may thus claw up the ground for a few yards only from fright on being shot at; but if not hurt, he would instantly resume his usual pace when making off. In this case his claws are always sheathed, nor are they ever protruded except for the purpose of striking its prey, or playfully tearing at tufts of long grass as they seem fond of doing, perhaps to clean their nails. At all other times the claws are completely hidden and protected. They would soon become blunt and worn down if used at all in walking. To alight on the hard dry ground after each bound with the claws thus extended, the men declared would greatly jar the tiger. We had cause two or three times afterwards to notice this fact, and felt sure a shot had told well, even though no blood could be found, if the ground was scratched for any great distance. It was proved in two cases when the tigers were both found dead, shot through the liver, after running about 300 yards at most.

CHAPTER XIV.

A WOODCUTTER DE TROP—FOUR BEARS AT ONCE—LOSE ALL—DRIVEN OFF BY THE BEES—EXCITE THE BUFFALO—TOO CLOSE BY HALF—REFLECTIONS ON PIG "SHOOTING"—OBSTINATE AS A BEAR—CHASE AND LOSE TWO TIGERS—AN ODD STYLE OF FISHING—NOT AT HOME—DEFEATED BY A BEAR—PRECAUTIONS IN FOLLOWING UP—BURNING OUT—A PRUDENT RESOLVE.

ON the 10th May, I found myself at "Balageer," a ravine in the plains, but as it yielded no sport, I walked across country six miles to "Palasiree" ravine, where we were told that a tiger had just killed a bullock. Before the beating began, I heard a man cutting wood a short distance from me, so I left my position on a large rock to warn him away, lest the tiger being wounded only should attack him in its flight. Just as I had returned to my place, to my great annoyance, the noise of this man's axe was again heard a little beyond; so fearing he might get killed (the blame of which accident would be sure to rest with me), I once more ran to order him to run away or climb a tree until the beating was over While returning to my other guns, as quick as possible, for the noise of the beaters had already commenced, having only my double rifle with me at the time, I heard a stone move, and directly saw a very large tiger moving off through the bushes at the foot of a low bank about twenty yards distant. I gave him one shot in the ribs, whereupon he bounded on into the dense jungle around, and was out of sight before I could fire my second barrel. After waiting until the men came up, we began following up the blood for about two hundred yards, when some Bheels placed on the look-out up trees saw this tiger get up out of a patch of high grass just before us, and make off across an open plain. We never saw the beast at all, owing to the long grass. It was too late now to attempt following up any longer, for the tent was a good seven miles off, and it was now just five o'clock. While hastening to warn away the man cutting wood, I twice passed close by a cave in which this tiger must have been lying hid. Most likely the beast was asleep. Had I been in my place on his first turning out of the den at the noise of the beaters, no doubt he would have been killed.

Having ordered my baggage on to "Deypoora," nine miles, I again went next morning to look for the tiger wounded yesterday, but found all the jungle around on fire, so there was no chance of finding him. Next tried the covers in the river at "Deypoora," but they were blank. Camels not up till very late, owing to bad rocky roads and steep hill to ascend.

Beat "Lonee" ravine on the 12th May. Only a bear turned out, which I killed with the first shot. Heard of a man being lately killed by a tiger in a ravine named "Manajee," near this place, and went next day to hunt there. Almost directly the beating began, a bear passed by where I was lying hid; I fired and wounded him severely with three shots. Just now a terrible noise was heard among the beaters, who were collected together outside the cover, while many had climbed up trees, having left off beating. I much feared that somebody had been hurt, for the roaring of a tiger was also heard, so I hastened to the spot, carrying three double rifles (two slung across my shoulders, and one in hand) up a very steep hill; very hard work this. The men told me there was a tiger still in the cover, but he positively refused to move for them, lying close in a large thick "corinda" bush. On their nearing this, he set up such a roar that there was a slight panic, for the men knew this brute to be a "man-eater." I quickly went round to another point of the cover, and seeing which way the wind was blowing, directed the long dry grass to be set on fire.

Shortly afterwards, two men up trees saw this tiger creep out over the hill-top up a small gully or watercourse, but from my position he could not be seen. The ground above the hills was too stony to "pug him up" over any distance, so we lost the brute. Next tried to follow up the wounded bear, but he had also escaped. The weather was quite cool all to-day.

I ordered off the kit to "Doraee," eight miles. On the way I beat "Mhadeo Kullah," a very extensive ravine full of "mowra" trees. The first part of the cover was blank, but at the next drive four large bears turned out at once. One bolted up the steep sides of the ravine and so escaped, for I was too busy attending to his friends. My eight barrels were divided among the lot; one bear remained dead on the field, but the two others made off—both badly wounded—into some very thick high grass. I fired at only about twenty yards' distance, so could not miss a shot. There were plenty of tracks, but a storm with heavy rain now came on very suddenly, and we did not attempt to follow up these wounded bears. All my guns, tent, servants, and self, were regularly soaked by this storm.

On the 16th of May, I walked four miles across the plains to "Adahallah" ravine, and beat the whole cover in one drive. Presently I saw a tiger bolting off over a perfectly open space, about a hundred yards distant; fired, but could not tell whether the bullets hit or not, for these shots turned out the confounded bees, of which there were many swarms about on the high rocks that formed the sides of this ravine. We all had to leave the place as fast as possible; several of the men got very badly stung.

Sent the tent on to "Jaat" on the 17th, while I went to beat a beautiful cover called "Loharees Kanuddee," having heard that a bullock had been lately killed there. We had gone almost through this thicket, which was very dense jungle indeed, without finding anything, when within about three yards only of the end, a fine tiger jumped up with loud roars, and bolted back through the beaters. I fired two shots, and afterwards found that they had told, by the quantity of blood about. It was here that we missed one of the men, and greatly feared he had been carried off or killed by this tiger; but to our great joy this lazy fellow shortly afterwards joined us, having lagged behind to smoke.

The cover was so thick that it was very dangerous to attempt following up this tiger, for we might have stepped on him before being able hardly to see him; nor was there room even to use a gun. While debating what was to be done under these circumstances, a large herd of buffaloes came down to drink at a stream close by, so we drove these animals into the thick patch of willow bushes, of which this cover was chiefly composed. The buffaloes evidently smelt the tiger, for they became greatly excited, and rushed forward in a body, crashing down all before them; while we followed in their path, and found by the blood that the tiger had passed on to another jungle a little further off. We lost this brute after all.

Having moved on to "Dowlutpoora" village, in the hope of being joined by Lieutenant Little for a month's sport, I here received a letter which, to my disappointment, stated that he could not obtain "leave of absence" for the purpose; so I sent the camels on to "Gwalior" Fort, six miles, and then started to beat "Bahara" ravine.

Suddenly there was a tremendous row among the beaters; one of them had accidentally struck a tiger that was moving on just in front of them, without their being aware of his presence, with a large stone (which they continue throwing on all sides as they advance while beating). The tiger at once turned round, and with fearful roars rushed back past the men, who were luckily at the time well together, so no harm was done. This was very provoking, for a few more yards would have brought him past the rock on which I was lying in wait—the same place from which Little and myself killed the tigress that so mauled one of our Bheels last year.

We next tried to beat this beast past in the opposite direction, for which purpose I changed my position to the other end of the ravine; but he refused to move or show himself, roaring loudly at the men. After firing many shots at random into the cover, but without any effect, I was obliged to leave the place; for it was too green to burn. This tiger, being much enraged, would most likely have hurt some of us in such a thick patch of jungle. He was hid among a lot of high green reeds, but the exact spot we could not tell.

For the next eight days, chiefly owing to the cool, wet weather, I saw no "large game" whatever, and merely killed a few sambur for their skins' sake. By this time I had moved round by short marches to "Koree" village. The Bheels there told me of another cover about four miles distant. We set out to beat it. On the road we saw some hog, at which the men wished me to fire for them to eat, but I would not, for fear of frightening away any wild beast that might be lying up in the neighbourhood. In such cool weather the least noise would have scared them miles away. In a rocky, hilly country, where it would be utterly impossible to ride hog, there was no great harm in occasionally shooting them for food. Otherwise, to talk of shooting pig on any ground where it is possible for a horse to move out of a walk, is a species of profanity, not to be tolerated in the eyes of any Indian sportsman. They rightly regard a hog, in places where there is the very faintest hope of being able to ride and spear them, as a kind of sacred animal, by reason of the heavenly sport they afford, and venerate him accordingly. Even as the English fox-hunter detests the man who traps, poisons, or shoots foxes in a hunting country, so does the "pig-sticker" in India regard any one who shoots a boar as guilty of a worse crime than sacrilege; always supposing that the boar could have been "speared" in a legitimate manner, which entirely depends upon the nature of the ground where he may be met with.

Soon after the men began beating this cover, there was a great uproar among them, occasioned by two large bears that were started, and persisted in breaking back past the beaters, in spite of the noise and blank shots fired to prevent them. Bears are often very obstinate on this point. Nothing will turn them from a given direction, but on they rush at a rough, shuffling pace, charging all before them. On one occasion I remember seeing the back and legs of a man much marked by the claws of a bear that had scampered over him. Finding it impossible to turn back this bear, several beaters, of whom this man was one, had very properly thrown themselves flat on their faces, so as to admit of the brute's passing them by unobserved, which, in his headlong flight, he did, only he unluckily happened to step rather roughly over this poor fellow lying down in his path.

The Bheels continued beating the remainder of this cover, when, presently, a fine tiger appeared, creeping along very cautiously just in front of the men. I meant to have allowed it to pass by my post as usual, but every now and then it stopped in the long grass to look around; when within about thirty yards it caught sight of me, so I was obliged to fire at once, as it stood still staring intently to make me out more clearly. The tiger instantly dropped to my shot at his head; nor could I see whereabouts it was lying, on account of the high grass covering its body. Hearing me fire so close, the men at once jumped up the nearest trees, of which there were plenty about. Here they remained in clusters of five and six up each slight tree. All being safe, I now fired another shot at random where I had last seen the tiger. Up it jumped in a moment, and with loud roars rushed back through the cover where the men had just been beating, but I fired three other shots before it was out of sight, for it was much crippled, having one fore leg broken, which it held up in its flight. We now, all together, began taking up the tracks in a body. There were a great quantity where the tiger had first fallen. Here, too, oddly enough, we discovered a broken tusk, so my ball had struck too low in the beast's jaw instead of its brain. We easily followed up the blood for half a mile or more, when all of a sudden it entirely ceased on open stony ground. We looked in all the little patches of grass or low bushes around, but could nowhere find any signs of this wounded tiger. To make matters worse, a sudden heavy shower of rain now began to fall, so it was hopeless attempting to hunt for the brute any longer. Just before this rain fell there were large clots of wet blood on the ground, so the tiger must have been moving only a little before us when the blood so unaccountably ceased altogether. Spots of blood dry the moment they fall to the ground, and are almost directly afterwards surrounded by numbers of extremely minute ants, that are at once attracted by the smell. From this it is easy to judge whether the game has passed on very lately, or some time before. Insect life in India is everywhere so infinite that there are always plenty of such signs to be found. Going homewards, I shot a blue bull for the men to eat.

I walked five miles across to "Ambah" on the 28th, in the hope of getting a shot at the tiger Little and myself had hunted there two years before. Soon after the men began beating this cover, a large bear turned out a few yards only from my position; but I did not fire at him. Thinking that the tiger, if there was one in the cover, would not be likely to "break" at the same place, I unluckily turned round, and watched another point of this thick jungle. Soon afterwards a slight noise at my back caused me to look round, when I saw a fine tiger bounding across an open space about forty yards from me, he having rushed out of the self-same spot that the bear did. I fired as quickly as possible, when the tiger roared to both shots, then suddenly turned off, and regained the cover, before another gun could be brought to bear upon him. After waiting until the men came up, we all together went to look for his prints; the ground was much marked by the tiger's claws at each long leap he took, but not a drop of blood could we find. Hoping he might still be in the cover, I now went about a mile ahead further up this ravine, while the men were told to try and again start the brute, but to beat the cover merely from the outside for fear of accidents, for we all felt pretty sure this tiger was wounded, though he could not be counted so, as no blood could be found. Had I only kept a look-out for him as at first, being more prepared, I must have killed him.

This second attempt to dislodge the tiger was a failure. We soon met a number of Bheels who were disturbing the cover by fishing in the low shallow stream of water that flowed through this long ravine. For the purpose of taking the same fish, these men had, at one part, almost dammed up the water where a few of them watched, while the rest advanced in a line from a long way up the stream, beating the water with boughs to drive on the fish. They had cut down a great quantity of "toor," or milk bush, to poison the fish: this bush thrown on the water had the effect of causing the fish to turn up their bellies, and float almost dead at the top of the water, when they were quickly taken out, and washed in clean water, being then none the worse for the poison. Baskets full of small fish were thus caught. Having a long walk back, I was now obliged to leave this cover; on the road I shot a "chinkara" or gazelle for dinner.

While marching with my camels on the 29th, we heard at a village that some woodcutters, who were clearing clumps of bamboos in the jungle, had just seen a tiger lying in a cave. I at once went with them to the spot, directing the kit to be sent on to "Nungpoora" village, ten miles from "Chuldoo." On arriving at the den the tiger was not at home, but there were plenty of his hairs about, so it was true he had been there. In the "hot season," when tigers shed their coats, they seldom lie down anywhere without leaving a few loose hairs to mark where their bed has been. At this time of the year the coat is very short indeed, but during the rains, or cold weather, the hair grows three times as long, and in this state a skin looks far more handsome. I tried several small, likely patches of jungle about, but could not find the beast.

Next day I went to beat a ravine named "Jerriah," full of willow-trees and high grass. While going ahead with a man carrying my spare guns, to take up my position before the beating began, I suddenly came upon a bear lying in a bush close by the path. She turned out at once, only a few yards off, so I was obliged to fire both barrels of my rifle. This brought the bear round on me sharp. I ran back to the man with the other loaded guns, who was about twenty paces behind me, but seeing the bear coming, in his fright he clutched the guns so tightly that I could not get hold of one even, so ran on further. On seeing the man, this bear made straight for him, when he dropped the guns quickly enough, and dived among some long grass with lightning speed. I presently saw the bear pass by growling awfully. She went near where the rest of the beaters were waiting to beat this cover, but they shouted and turned her off. They declared she had a cub on her back, but in my hurry I did not notice it. On picking up my guns I found the barrels full of wet sand, so had to clean them before hunting.

On 31st May, I walked from this place over to "Oomurchee," a small town four miles off, where the Bheels had promised to try and mark down a tiger for me that had lately killed many of their cattle; but oddly enough, they declared that he was now nowhere to be found, though many men had been looking out for him. This did not prevent me from beating all the likely places about, which these men readily enough pointed out. After visiting about a dozen of his haunts—caves, good shady covers, and many patches of high grass in the plains, where a tiger would not hesitate to lie during this cool weather—we were returning to the village in despair, when I determined to try one other small piece of jungle, chiefly composed of long grass and low thorn-bushes, close to the walls of "Oomurchee." Here, much to my surprise, the tiger at once appeared, on the first blank shot of the beaters. I tried hard to get a clear shot at his head as he trotted past, about forty yards off, but the ball struck him in the neck instead. The next bullet hit somewhere about his shoulder, when, with loud roars, he sprang up a sloping bank on my right and disappeared in the thick jungle. I could only get one other shot at him, but most likely missed, being in a great hurry. The Bheels now came up and we began following up his blood, quantities of which had spirted out on both sides, sprinkling the rocks, bushes, and grass, as he bounded off. We silently followed for at least a mile and a half, every moment expecting to view the game, for he had gone across quite an open plain, where the grass had lately been burnt, and seemed from the small pools of blood about to have pulled up under many bushes. But it soon became too dusk to follow any longer, so we were obliged to leave this brute and return home. He was found dead two days afterwards.

From the number of precautions one is absolutely compelled to take in "following up," the pace is necessarily very slow. Men having to be sent up trees to look out, every thirty or fifty yards, the rest waiting below till they descend, so that all may keep together. Constant attention to see that nobody loiters behind to smoke, &c., as well as having to track the marks or blood (in this case easy enough), keeping a bright look-out on all sides, in case of a charge, and seeing that the spare guns are close at hand. Stopping every now and then to throw a stone in some likely looking bush and watching the effect—all these little acts cause some delay, by which many a wounded beast gets clear off for the time. But prudence demands it, otherwise accidents would be very frequent, when such hunting would cease to be sport at all, and become mere risk of life. As it is, there is quite excitement enough in the chase, however cautiously conducted. This was a very large tiger, with an enormous footprint.

Ordered off the kit to "Janodeep," a village six miles distant. On the way I discovered a beautiful cover, called "Goodalee," full of high green reeds, dry grass, corindas, bamboo clumps, &c., with plenty of water about. The men started a bear from this ravine, but I did not see it. There was also plenty of fresh tiger-prints found. Rather to my surprise, this splendid piece of jungle twice proved blank; but while we were returning to the tent we saw at a bend of the road a fine tiger drinking at a small pool of water about ninety yards in front. I fired both barrels of my rifle as he began to walk away on seeing us, and made him roar. He now gallopped off into a long patch of high grass a little farther on; so, taking three guns with me, I ran ahead about three hundred yards, making a great circuit towards a low tree at the end of this strip of high grass, into which I climbed quietly as possible. Before leaving the rest of the men behind, I had told them to wait a little, so as to give me time to get well ahead, and then to begin beating. I was no sooner up the tree than they began making a noise, even before there was time for me to reach up my spare guns. Almost directly afterwards this tiger came slowly creeping out of the long grass, but he at once stopped and looked full at me, for the tree was very bare, having no leaves to hide me. He instantly got a shot in his chest, which doubled him for half a moment, but he sprang back again into the high grass before another shot could be fired, and went roaring terribly towards a low bank on which the beaters were standing together. On hearing my shot and this noise, the men at once climbed trees that were close by. After waiting a few minutes, we called out to each other. None of the Bheels had seen the tiger go by; so we knew he was lying somewhere in the high grass. I now got out of my tree, and went round to the men. We next, leaving a few up trees on the look-out, examined the spot where I had fired, and found plenty of blood. Suddenly one of the men, by a low whistle, drew our attention to the tiger, standing by a tree just on the edge of the cover, at about thirty yards' distance. He seemed much confused, and never looked even towards us, but had his head bent down to the ground. I waited to let the men get more together, or up trees, for safety, and was just about to fire, when the beast slowly walked back into the grass. Here he could be nowhere again seen, although we climbed the highest trees overlooking this cover. It was now getting dark, so I at once set fire to the grass at both ends of the long strip or patch of thick jungle, which was about a hundred yards in length, by fifty wide. The fire raged beautifully, and had nearly met within ten yards, when thinking the tiger must be dead, or he never would lie so close, I walked forward in the hope of saving his skin, when within certainly not more than twelve paces, up the brute jumped with an awful roar (which I certainly never shall forget, for it seemed to lift me off my legs—going in at the soles of my boots and out of the top of my hunting cap like an electric shock) and sprang back through the flames, which had now nearly met. I fired one shot in what seemed the right direction, as he bounded off, but it really was too dark to see anything distinctly, and the smoke of the burning grass shut out all view beyond. The beast had been lying, completely hid, in a small deep ditch in the middle of this patch of grass, which accounted for our not being able to see him from above. He was found dead the next day, but I lost the skin, having to ride on, late as it was, to "Kooakhera," six miles, with a terrible steep ghaut or hill to descend. It was afterwards discovered that this tiger had just killed a bullock when we first met him drinking at the pool. The Bheels of this village declared that three or four men had been killed by tigers here while tending their cattle during the past year.

The fright I got to-day was a good lesson never to advance alone under any circumstances whatever; but having fired several shots into this very spot from the high trees around, and seeing how sick the tiger seemed when we last saw him, besides knowing that my first bullet must have raked him well, I could not but suppose him dead. Instead of which he went off very lively indeed. My men did not join me till next morning with the guns, in the plains below.

Here I heard that two officers of the "Kotah Contingent" had just left this place, having killed a bear in a large ravine among the hills, where they had hunted with two elephants. It was very cool to-day, so I gave the men a rest, and merely took a walk after cleaning up my "battery." During my walk I shot a four-horned deer or "beadlah," and a murrel fish, twenty-two inches long, in the river there; so we were well off for food.

CHAPTER XV.

Grain carriers—A panic—A buck in a fix—Bees again—Continued ill-luck—"Eyes in the dark"—A prudent bear—Taken in the rear—A lucky escape—Kill the tiger—Dacoits—Murrel and snipe—The last hunt—The bag.

Only thirteen days of my term of leave now remained. On the 2nd of June, I set out to beat the "Booj" ravine, three miles distant, but to my annoyance found it full of cattle belonging to some "Brinjaree" people—a wandering race who live by carrying grain, &c., from place to place by means of their numerous bullocks, which are hired by native merchants for the purpose. A number of the small tents of these people were pitched close by the cover, so it was useless to try for game there. We, therefore, walked across to "Putloee" ravine, four miles; but to my disgust this place was also crowded by another set of these men, with an immense herd of cattle, which they were driving down to drink at this cover. The beaters had been sent on with orders to begin beating lower down the ravine, while I branched off with one man carrying the spare guns to this point of the cover. There was no time to send back and stop the beating, so I begged and warned the cattle-owners to drive back their cattle from this cover. They, however, paid no attention whatever to me. The noise of the beaters was now heard at a good distance off, so I ran about a hundred yards towards them, and waited over the ravine. Presently a fine tigress, followed by a half-grown cub, passed below my post. I gave the tigress one ball in the ribs, at which she roared and rushed past out of sight into some very thick high green reeds. The cub stood still, seemingly much astonished, so I "peppered" him well with three barrels before he followed his mother's steps. A most laughable scene then took place, for the herd of bullocks, hearing the tigress come roaring down towards them, were at once seized with a panic, and set off full tilt up the ravine, which was very narrow just here, upsetting their owners, who in vain endeavoured to stop their flight. There were at least three hundred bullocks racing off at their utmost speed, tails up high in the air, for about three or four hundred yards, when an opening in the deep ravine allowed them to escape across the open plain above, over which they scattered themselves, still going their best pace in a fearful state of alarm. One poor beast was left behind, having been knocked down and trampled on by the rest, whereby its leg was broken. The "Brinjarees," on hearing the tiger's roars, also hastened out of the cover and jumped up the trees on the banks above, where they remained for some time. The tigress had pulled up a little short of where the cattle were drinking in some very thick reeds. I fired many shots at random, but could not again put her out. It would not have been safe to look for her in such awfully thick jungle, slightly wounded, and, moreover, enraged as she was at having her cub shot.

We left the ravine for the tent. All being quiet, the cattle-owners descended from their trees, and with much abuse clamoured to be paid for the lame bullock; but as they had wilfully neglected my repeated cautions, and, moreover, caused me to lose these two tigers—for there was no time to take up a proper position before the beating began, as I had wasted so long trying to persuade these men to remove their beasts, which they could easily have done—none of the Bheels nor I could see what right they had to be paid. We did not get home till long after dark, having many miles to walk.

Moved on the baggage to "Limree," five miles, on the

5th. Went over to "Kokee" ravine, and beat the whole of it, but it proved blank. We were obliged to retreat from this cover on account of the bees; many of the men were badly stung. Going homewards I shot a fine buck "cheetul;" and while following up his prints and blood as silently as possible, in the hope of getting another shot on our again starting him, we heard a great stamping and crashing of bushes about forty yards ahead; soon we saw the buck trying to shake off a large jackal, that had pinned him by the throat. The cheetul in vain tried, by swinging his head backwards and forwards violently, to dislodge the jackal, who, doubled up like a ball, held on as well as the best bull-dog could have done. Nor did he loose his hold, until, after watching this strange scene for some minutes, I dropped the "cheetul" with another shot. The jackal hastily retreated. This jackal had, no doubt, smelt the blood of the wounded deer, as it passed where he must have been lying down during the day. Often, when walking after a wounded black buck or antelope in the plains, I have seen one or two jackals trotting along in the exact direction the wounded deer had gone off. The wind, no doubt, carried the scent of blood past the bushes in which these jackals hide themselves in the day-time. There is thus little chance of any wounded small animal escaping these watchful creatures.

During the next two days I got no sport, except some small deer, and a sambur. On the third, while beating "Manajee" ravine, opposite "Morwun" village, where my tent had been sent, a small tiger was seen in the cover, but I could not get a shot at the cub, the jungle being so thick. We walked over to "Banda," a cover four miles off above the hills, in which a tiger was said to live that had killed three men this year. We beat the whole place most carefully, but could not find the beast. The weather was still very cool, so the tiger could lie out anywhere.

On the morning of the 9th a swarm of bees turned out and attacked everybody. We were obliged to leave the tent and baggage, and run for it some distance off. Where these bees came from, or why, nobody could tell, for there were none near where we were encamped. My guns had luckily been sent forward, so I followed them, well muffled up, but got slightly stung.

We beat the covers in the river close by, but saw no tiger, although a bullock had been killed there overnight. I now walked over to "Mhadee Kullah," five miles beyond "Ruthinghur" fort. Before beating this splendid ravine, I went silently with two men, carrying the spare guns, to look at a deep cave we knew in which a tiger was said to live. Standing quite quiet against the rocks, on one side of the entrance, we threw in about a dozen small stones, in the hope of getting a shot at the tiger as he rushed out down the hill near the top of which this den was situated. Nothing came out, so we concluded the cave must be empty, and next walked round to the other side of this large ravine, posting ourselves on a rock directly opposite the cave. Here I signed, by waving my cap to the beaters who were waiting below the hill, to begin making a noise. Scarcely had they done so, when, to the inexpressible astonishment of the Bheels with me, as well as myself, a magnificent tiger slowly crawled out of the very den we had just been stoning. The distance was over 200 yards; I fired two shots, but both fell short just at his feet, when, with loud roars, he rushed off in the dense jungle, and was soon out of sight. This tiger seemed by far the largest I had ever seen. Both the men with me said they mistook him at first for a sambur when seen indistinctly moving through some thick brushwood. We looked for this brute in two or three other covers adjoining, but he had gone off altogether. Never was such ill luck as this. Had he only turned out on our first quietly throwing in the stones,

I must have shot him, being so close. The camels did not reach this place till nearly midnight, for it was impossible to approach the tent, or pack the baggage, until sunset, on account of the bees; some of my servants were badly stung.

On the 12th June, having ordered my kit on to "Panghur" fort, the usual place of commencing and ending the season's sport, I went to once more beat the "Bahara" ravine on the road there. This beautiful cover proved blank, although some cattle had been lately killed in this neighbourhood. When the men had finished beating the ravine, I determined to walk through the place and explore the numerous caves in it, so as to know how to act on a future occasion, several beasts having baffled us at this cover, refusing to show themselves in spite of our utmost efforts to drive them out of their strongholds. After looking into two or three deep caves, I came to one rather shallow. Here I saw something sparkling at the far end of it, like a fire-fly. Silently pointing it out to my chief "huntsman," he was some time before observing what I meant, for every now and then the dim greenish light was somehow extinguished. Then it would again shine forth clearly enough. We were talking in a low tone of voice about this odd circumstance, standing all the while immediately in the mouth of the cave, with the rest of the men grouped behind us, when my "shikaree" quietly pressed my arm, and whispered that it was a tiger's eyes that we were looking at. This was pleasant indeed! Rather a hasty retreat was at once made, for the men saw by our signs of caution, as we stepped back, that something strange had been discovered. Quietly as possible we all went round, and stood guard over and above the entrance of this cave. Then a sudden noise of shouting, blank pistol shots, &c., was raised, with many stones thrown into the den. A low growling just under our feet was immediately heard in reply, when out rushed a large bear into the dense jungle in front of this cave: I fired both barrels of my rifle, which caused him to roar louder, when he was instantly out of sight, the high grass and reeds closing over him as he hastily retreated. We now began following up his tracks, and soon found him dead. Both balls had lodged in his back. He was very old indeed, which, perhaps, accounted for his behaving so cunningly. Had he only charged while we were looking into his den (in spite of my guns, for there would not have been time or room to use them), he must have upset the heap of us; at the very least, he would have mauled some of us severely, if not worse. We skinned him on the spot; and a dreadfully tough job it was. We then walked after the camels on the road to "Panghur." Just as we had overtaken them, I dismounted from my pony, and went to look at a deep cave a few score yards off the road side. Here I heard another bear growl, rather to the surprise of the men with me as well as myself; remembering our late adventure, there was a rush back for a few paces. We returned, but failed to dislodge this bear, in spite of a very large bonfire hastily formed of wood and dry grass collected close by, fired, and thrust into the cave. The heat of this fire was so great that large fragments of rock kept splitting off, and flying around with loud reports, such as I had never before seen or heard. But all was in vain, though the bear must have been well warmed. We followed the baggage, and got to our ground by dark.

In the morning, after first silently visiting a panther's cave, we began beating the steep hill-side, on which the ruined fort is built, for there is a quantity of dense brushwood and jungle on this hill, which forms a famous cover for "large game" of all sorts. Soon after the beating commenced, the men on the look-out, on a bare hill opposite, saw a tiger quietly leave the dense cover, and go over the hill-top (which was nearly bare and free from jungle), on the ridge of which I was lying down, keeping watch with my guns around me.

Presently the beaters, having met with this tiger's fresh prints, as he moved off, began firing double pistol shots in rapid succession to let me know what was coming. Much to my surprise, the men had arrived within about twenty yards of my post, without my being able to see any animal moving past, in the dense brushwood immediately below the steep rocky bank over the edge of which I was intently peering. I heard a slight noise behind, as if a stone had been gently moved; and on quietly looking round over my shoulder, saw to my great horror, a large tiger creeping past, as silently and cautiously as possible, within not more than five yards of my heels. The beast had evidently not observed me, while thus lying down so close to him, for my clothes were luckily of much the same colour as the rocks around. He seemed only intent on moving off unobserved by the beaters, who were just behind him; and was slowly crawling by, in the most stealthy manner possible, with his chin close to the ground and looking straight ahead. For a moment I did not even dare to breathe or make the slightest movement. To my intense joy, having passed on about twenty paces, the tiger began to slowly descend a sloping part of the hill-side beyond my post. Then, with a feeling that it was impossible to remain still for even one moment longer, I sprang up and began firing my guns with the utmost rapidity into this tiger. On receiving my first shot, so intent was he on silently getting out of this cover, that he turned round sharp, but merely uttered a faint sort of gasp, instead of the usual loud grunt with which tigers mostly acknowledge the receipt of a shot. My next bullet, about the shoulders, staggered him. In my haste and excitement the third missed altogether, but the fourth luckily upset him, while the two other guns prevented him again getting on his legs. My men, on hearing these shots so close, quickly climbed up some small trees at hand. When they at length joined me, they owned to being much astonished, well knowing the exact spot where I was posted, at my having, as they thought, allowed the tiger to pass by without firing at him, for they did not know that the brute had broken cover above the hill-top, which really was an odd proceeding on his part, considering how open and free from cover of any sort the ground there was. These men all agreed that I had escaped in a most wonderful manner, and attributed it to my not moving in the least, as well as the fact of my whole dress so much resembling in colour the rocky ground on which I was lying. My guns were all turned the wrong way when the tiger passed, so there would have been no time even to use them, considering how close he passed me. His prints, which were very large, would have plainly showed his course; yet, but for the accidental moving of a stone, this tiger would have escaped me. He measured eleven feet ten inches long, and was very stout.

At night some rogues paid my little encampment a visit, but the dogs gave timely warning. One had a lighted matchlock; but on my turning out to see what was the matter, they ran off. The thief with the gun could easily have been shot, for in the dark night his lighted match betrayed the way he fled. These fellows had robbed some people of this village of their ornaments, and had stolen a cow besides, with which they got clear off. There was much lamentation next morning on the part of the losers. There seemingly were a few of these rascals about this part of the country; for, on a former occasion, we once met, near this place, a "buniar," or grain merchant, and his son, with three or four women howling terribly by the road-side. On inquiry, they told us that some thieves had just stopped their bullock-cart, and with many blows and threats had robbed them of their goods, afterwards disappearing over the steep hills covered with thick bushes close by. The poor women had been sadly treated, for their noses and ears, from which their ornaments and jewels had been forcibly torn, were bleeding profusely. These robbers, however, were unarmed, but those who had been pillaged by them spoke in high terms of the dexterity with which the rogues threw stones, and showed many bruises as proof of their skill.

I shot some fine "murrel" fish the next day, in the large lake or tank here. They were very plentiful, but will not readily bite at any sort of bait. Once, when snipe-shooting over this very piece of water, in the "cold season," I lost two birds that dropped in the water a few yards only from the shore. Much to my wonder, each time a large fish instantly rose and took down the snipe that had but just fallen, without seeming to care for the report of the gun. Seeing this game, I quickly borrowed a large hook from some of our pic-nic party, who were fishing, and then cutting down a long bamboo as a rod, soon fastened a small bird, shot for the purpose, as bait to the line of string, and began trolling and whipping the water for a long distance until quite tired, without having however a single rise. But no sooner had I taken off the small bird from the hook and thrown it into the water, than a monster fish instantly swallowed this bait.

While breakfasting, a cowherd came running in to say that he had just seen a tiger in the very cover where I had killed one the day before. Collecting the Bheels, I hastened to take up the same position on the rocky ledge at top of the steep hill, previously warning two men to climb a high tree overlooking the point at which the tiger had yesterday escaped from the cover by ascending the hill. Should this beast attempt to play the same game, these men were to frighten it back into the dense cover below, by coughing, or making any slight noise. This they promised to do, and then left me alone, lying down as before at my post, with the "battery" close by my side. The noise of the beaters was soon afterwards heard, as, also, to my delight, the double pistol shots; but, strange to say, the men again came on close up, without any tiger having passed my post, in spite of the bright look-out I kept both in front and rear. The beaters declared they had once seen the tiger, but could not make out where it had gone. We returned together, and began taking up its footprints, when, to my intense disgust, we found that this tiger had actually walked off up the very same path or tract by which the other had passed. It now appeared that the lazy fellows I had directed to guard this outlet, and had even pointed out the very tree up which they were to climb, had failed to occupy the post, preferring to accompany the rest of the beaters. We tried hard to continue following up the prints, but the ground soon became so stony that it was impossible. After looking over every likely patch of jungle for miles round, but in vain, I was obliged to return home to the tent.

I was cruelly annoyed at the worse than carelessness of these two men; for if they had in the least objected to watch that particular point, I should have myself done so, and must have easily killed this other tiger. Not knowing the exact spot in which he was hiding, I preferred going a long way ahead, so as to have the benefit of the whole length of the cover. It never answers to beat a place in two drives, taking up a fresh position, as the beaters have finished the first half of any jungle; for if the game should happen to be lying at the farthest end of the long cover, it would most likely at once be off on hearing the noise of the men beating the first part. It is a far better plan to have one long drive, stationing men up trees to guard all the likely points at which the game may break cover. My "leave of absence" had now expired. The baggage was sent into camp, while I had a final look for the tiger that so unfortunately escaped me on the 14th; but his prints were not again to be found; and, unloading the guns, I rode back to Camp Neemuch, getting well soaked by rain on the road.

This season's "bag" would most likely have been larger

had the weather not proved so wet and cool. The following animals composed it—viz., nine tigers killed, eight tigers wounded; three bears killed, and twelve bears wounded; total, thirty-two head of "large game" killed and wounded, besides several deer of different sorts.

CHAPTER XVI.

1853—EARLY IN THE FIELD—FIRST SHOT—MEET A COMRADE—UNPROPITIOUS WEATHER—AN OLD STAGER—AN ADVENTUROUS PANTHER—SET ON FIRE!—FOUR TIGERS—USE OF POCKET GLASSES—A SURPRISE—LOSE THE GAME.

IN 1853 I set out betimes. As soon as I had applied for a three months' leave, I obtained leave for ten days in anticipation—a sort of preface to the regular sport of the year. I rode out from Camp Neemuch on the 13th March, and reached Jaat, where my baggage had already been sent on. It was rather early in the season to commence hunting, for as yet the hot weather had scarcely begun. Everywhere the jungle had a very thick appearance. The leaves had not yet fallen from the trees, and the vegetation had not become withered up by the sun. It was difficult in most places to see even a few yards ahead, which, consequently, greatly increased the chances against being able to discover wild beasts; and, instead of their being forced to seek only particular spots for shade and shelter, the whole country afforded them equally good cover. It was three days before I came upon any "large game," having, in the meantime, only shot some sambur for the leather sake.

On 16th March, while beating "Bahara" ravine, having taken up my old position on the low sloping bank, a tiger soon appeared. I allowed him to pass by before firing, when he stopped still to listen to the noise of the men behind him; so I got a good shot at the back of his neck, only fifteen paces off, and rolled him over. He instantly recovered his legs, and, with loud roars, sprang back past me into the cover, from which he had just emerged. I fired three other shots as he bolted off, some of which told. But now a difficulty occurred; for having only eight or nine men with me, I much feared to enter into the dense jungle in search of the wounded tiger, lest he should hurt some of us. As we were such a small party, the beast would hardly hesitate to charge us.

Next day, having collected more Bheels from "Dowlutpoora" village, near there, we again looked for this wounded tiger, but he had left the cover altogether in the meantime. While looking about to-day in this jungle, I saw a beautiful civet cat, the first of the kind yet met with in this part of the country. In the evening rode on to "Panghur" fort with my baggage.

Here I met Capt. A——, 1st Bombay Lancers, who was out here for a few days' fishing; and agreed to beat all the covers about with him on the following morning. We began beating the steep hill on which the fort is built. Unluckily, we had both posted ourselves up a tree overlooking the path by which two tigers had last year left the thick cover below and gone over the hill-top. Presently a fine tiger was seen coming on through the bushes, but, unfortunately, at the very bottom of the hill; so we had to fire long shots, as he was quite a hundred yards off. One of A——'s barrels missed fire, but we felt sure that some of the remaining three shots had told. The tiger quickly slunk into the thick jungle, and was no more seen. We now went down with all the men to look for blood, but could find none. A day or two afterwards, we again tried to find this tiger, having been assured by some cowherds that they had seen the beast crawl out of a cave near where we fired at him, very lame indeed. In the cave we found some of his hair, but could nowhere put up the tiger himself, although we looked in every likely place about here. I afterwards heard that he was killed by some chiefs, not two miles from this village; but that he managed to kill one man, and maul another sadly, who had tried to find out where he was hiding, after having been fired at by these chiefs. They found two of our bullets in his body. I had unluckily dissuaded A—— from taking up a separate position in the cover below, as he much wished to do, or we must have "bagged" this tiger easily.

I walked across to "Bahara" ravine, six miles, the next day; and this time climbed up a small tree in the very midst of this terribly dense cover. Soon I caught a glimpse of a tiger moving among some reeds a few yards off, but could not fire at the time. He would not leave the cover, so I took up another position, and then the men tried to drive him in the opposite direction, but in vain. There were only thirteen of us altogether, so this ravine could only be imperfectly beaten from the outside; for it would have been very dangerous for so few men to enter such a thick cover. Most likely this tiger remained hid in some of the numerous caves about. He would not turn out, although we set fire to as much of the grass as would burn. Obliged to leave the tiger alone, and return home to my tent at "Panghur."

Next morning, having ridden about a mile on my way back to camp, for my ten days' leave was up, a cowherd came running after me to say that a tiger had just killed one of his cows, so I at once returned to the place he pointed out. There was the bullock, quite warm and whole, the tiger having merely sucked its blood. Feeling sure the brute must be lying up somewhere close by, I went ahead, while a few men, hastily collected, began beating some patches of jungle near at hand. No tiger appeared; and again I started for camp, and got there by dark.

On the 26th March I returned to my tent left at "Panghur," having, in the meantime, obtained my expected "leave of absence." Here I was told that, at night, the tiger we had last looked for, had returned and eaten the dead bullock, and was yesterday seen by some woodcutters to walk from under a solitary "corinda" bush, far out in the plain, away from other jungle, and close by a high road too. Very cunning beast this, to hide in such an unlikely place, but the cool weather allowed game to lie out anywhere. I stopped two more days, looking in every possible corner for this tiger, but in vain, for the Bheels there were very anxious that he should be killed; as, for a long time past, they had lost a bullock regularly every third or fourth day.

For the next eleven days, although I marched over a great extent of ground where formerly good sport could be had, no "large game" gladdened my eyes. Fresh prints of tigers, panthers, and bears, were, in many places, plentiful enough; but we could nowhere find even one. This was chiefly owing to the weather, which continued so mild, and the frequent showers of rain that fell. At one place, I was shown a deserted hut that stood alone in the jungle. Here the Bheels assured me a large panther had made a great hole (still visible) in the thatch by which he entered to kill some goats that were penned up within the hut, although, at the time, there were two men also living there. They were quite unarmed, and could offer no opposition; therefore, they hid themselves in a large empty wicker basket, usually kept to hold grain in until the panther took himself off, after having killed several of the goats.

While at Jaat, having tracked a tiger into some deep iron-pits, we made a grand bonfire of dry grass and wood in the mouth of one of the caves, over which I kept guard, having sent my men to a short distance off. Presently I felt something prick my back, but for the moment fancied it might only be the thorns of a thick bush by which I was standing. Again the pain, much sharper this time, made me wince; when, looking round, I found my woolly sort of coat was on fire! Some sparks from the bonfire, which blazed high up in the air, had fallen on me without being observed, for I was intently watching the cave, expecting every moment to see a singed tiger bolt out through the flames. Throwing down my rifle, I ran off, trying hard to disengage my powder-horn, which was slung across my shoulders and fastened to my belt. The men quickly came up, and at once put out the burning clothes, by covering me with their blankets as I rolled on the grass, which also caught fire. No harm was done, beyond some slight smarts and the fright I got. The tiger did not appear. These pits lead one into each other far under ground; so perhaps the fire was hardly felt within. Merely a few sambur and small deer were shot during this time; one of which, a little "beadlah," or four-horned ravine deer, that several times was started out of some long grass, was mistaken by a few of the men for a tiger, as it bounded away in front, while we silently followed it for some distance. Many of them swore to having seen its stripes most distinctly, until at last the joke was discovered. So a great deal of excitement was thrown away.

On the 8th April, I set out to beat the ravine near "Doraee" village, called "Bunsur," where a man herding cattle had been killed the day before; taking nineteen Bheels with me, besides my own men. Presently a terrible roaring of a tiger was heard; when, shortly afterwards, I was told that two tigers had broken back past the beaters, who, fortunately, were well together at the time. I at once changed my position for the far end of this cover, while the men once more began beating it in the opposite direction. Soon afterwards, on looking up, I saw four tigers quietly walking over the top of a steep hill that slopes down towards this ravine. They were about two hundred yards off; so I did not fire. Three of the tigers seemed full grown tigresses; but the fourth was a perfect monster, at least half as big again as either of the others. We now altogether tried to take up their prints, but the ground was much too rocky; so we followed in the direction the tigers had gone towards some caves. On nearing which a tigress bolted out at a great pace. Luckily I rolled her completely over by a ball in the neck; but the brute was soon up again, and crawled under some thick "corinda" bushes close by. We had much bother looking for her, but at last I caught a glimpse of where she was lying hid, about fifteen yards off; so fired as sharp as possible four shots into her. The beast jumped up with loud roars, but was too crippled to charge. Another bullet or two settled the business. She measured nine feet ten inches long. By the time we had skinned this tigress it was dusk.

Next morning, 9th April, some men came early to my tent to say that a tiger was roaring from the top of a hill overlooking the village of "Doraee," and that they could distinctly see him from below, lying on a rock. I went to the place; and there, with my pocket telescope (which was worn in a small leather case on my shoulder-belt, and invariably formed part of my hunting gear), I could clearly make out what seemed to be a very large tiger indeed. I was in hopes it might be the monster one seen yesterday not far from this village. My men, who were also acquainted with the use of the telescope, agreed that it was an immense tiger.

We most of us carried these small pocket-glasses, and found them of the greatest use, especially if looking over a hill-side for sambur. On one occasion I saw a fine buck lying under a small shady tree on the slope of a high hill, and pointed him out to the Bheels with me. But they all most positively declared that it was merely a large stone or piece of rock, and that they had known it to be there, some said, from their infancy, and others even before the small tree had grown up. Nevertheless I made a great circuit, and quietly gained the hill-top exactly over this supposed stone. It after all turned out to be a fine sambur; for he passed within a few yards of me, and was shot the moment the men roused him by making a noise below. They joked much with each other about the stone, as they divided the meat. They were either too lazy to help me get this animal, or had really mistaken it. Sambur, in the hot weather, change their coats to a greyish colour, and will lie, during the heat of the day, remarkably close under some shady tree, where there is a good look-out all round. It is then often difficult to distinguish them from any large stones or bits of rock scattered over the hill's side. But this is a digression.

We quickly determined on the following plan of operations for circumventing the tiger:—leaving some men below the hill, who by signs were to guide us in our course, I was, in company with my two "huntsmen" and a Bheel, carrying the spare guns and water bag, to go round, and, as silently as possible, ascend the hill from the opposite side. Then advance on tiptoe in rear of the tiger, and blow his brains out, before he should be aware of our presence. Very nicely we managed it; for after climbing the steep hill without making the faintest noise, we slowly walked forward, keeping a bright look out, and holding our breath. After going a few paces, we heard a loud roar just in our front, and directly afterwards came upon a fine panther, lying with his back towards us on a large rocky ledge that formed the summit of this hill. Fully expecting to see a tiger, I was so surprised that I never even thought of firing; when, suddenly, the panther turned round sharp, and at once crouched down as if about to spring. He was only about eight or ten paces off, so I at once banged at him without aiming at any particular mark, when he instantly disappeared over the edge of the precipice so swiftly that there was no time even to give him the second barrel. The ball had struck somewhere about its face, and had knocked the brute backwards, all of a heap. The men on the look-out below now set off, running as fast as they could along the bottom of the hill; so we followed in the same direction above, looking over the sides of the steep hill, for we fancied these men were merely running to keep the game in view; instead of which, it afterwards appeared that, seeing the panther thus tumble headlong down the hill-side, they fancied he was going to charge them, were seized with a panic, and ran off in what proved to be the wrong direction. On retracing our steps, we found that this panther had crawled off among some very thick brushwood on the other side of the hill, and entered a deep cave, from which we could not expel him. Very annoying to lose this skin through such a stupid mistake. What most puzzled us was how he ever could have been mistaken for so large a tiger; there must have been some haze in the atmosphere at the time.

Found no more game that day; but, the next, heard of a cow being killed by a tiger at "Sanda," a village only a mile distant. This news was brought me over night, and the next morning we went to the place, and found the cow half eaten. This made us feel certain of finding the tiger somewhere near at hand. Soon after, he turned out of the very first ravine we tried, but unluckily broke back over a steep hill instead of coming along a "nullah," or watercourse, over which I was keeping guard. I fired four shots at him as he bounded up the hill, beginning at about eighty yards. He acknowledged each shot with a roar; but, strange to say, on going to the spot, not one drop of blood could be found. We looked in several other large ravines near, for which this tiger seemed bound, but could nowhere again see him. From being unable to find blood, I do not count this tiger as wounded, but cannot help thinking he must have been hit.

CHAPTER XVII.

CAMPAIGNING IN FORCE—A POWERFUL BATTERY—MEET WITH ILL LUCK—BUT AT LENGTH FIND STORE OF GAME—FIVE TIGERS WOUNDED—FINDING THE KILLED—LAYING SIEGE — A PERILOUS NIGHT MARCH — SOME IDEA OF THE "HOT SEASON"—TAKE HOLIDAY—AN EXCITING INCIDENT—A HUNT IN THE DARK—STRENGTH OF THE PANTHER.

ON returning in the evening to my tent, I heard that the camels and baggage of my friends, Lieutenant Little and Lieutenants Forbes and Lock, both of 1st Bombay Lancers, had already arrived at "Ruttenghur Fort," four miles off. They had agreed to meet me there for six weeks' tiger hunting, during this year's hot season, for which purpose they had accordingly obtained leave of absence from Camp Neemuch. My servant, at once sent off on horseback, soon returned, confirming this news.

I found, at this time, that somehow I had missed counting a day. This same mistake once before happened to A. B. L—— and self, and serves to prove how delightfully the time passes at this sort of sport. Ordering my kit to follow me, I at once joined the party at "Ruttenghur."

For the next four days we hunted together, but found no "large game," although a man had been lately killed by a tiger in "Niliadeo Kullah," an extensive ravine, close by this place. In the meantime, we had moved on to the village of "Jawnda," eleven miles. On the fifth day, 16th April, we were told of a tiger at "Lohareea," a village a few miles off; so we went there with our guns and beaters, first sending the tents on to "Limree," six miles. On beating a thick patch of willow bushes that formed the cover, in the dry bed of a river, at this place, a young tiger was turned out and quickly murdered. We now retraced our steps, to beat another patch of jungle as yet untouched, and took up our position on a low bank on one side of the river, standing side by side, with our spare rifles laid on the ground at our feet. With such a formidable "battery," each man having three double guns or rifles, total, twenty-four shots, it was immaterial where we chose to stand; for we felt convinced no tiger could have a chance of doing mischief before such volleys as we could give him. And so it proved; for soon afterwards a fine tigress came bounding by our post, out of the thick cover. We allowed her to almost pass our front, when at a word she was knocked completely off her legs, and killed dead before half the guns had been fired. She had not time to even roar before being laid low a few yards from us in the bed of the river. We skinned her and the young one under a tree near the village and then rode on to our tents at "Limree." It afterwards appeared that there was yet another young tiger in this cover, but at the time we did not see him. A few days after his mother and sister had thus been killed, he attacked a goat, when the villagers rose in a body, chased him into a cave, and there literally roasted him alive. They seemed to consider this great fun. The tigress we shot here had just killed a cow, over which the vultures, as usual, had begun to assemble from all points. We pegged down the two skins by candle-light.

For the next thirteen days, during which time a good deal of rain fell, we unfortunately found no "large game" whatever, although we hunted every day from morning till evening. At one place only, named "Goodalee," was a tiger started by the men, but he at once left the beautiful cover, and walked over a stony open plain without our being able to see him. This he never could have done had the weather been hotter, for the rocks would have burnt his feet. A few sambur and small deer were all we shot in this time. By moving almost daily, we had now got to "Indoreghur" ravine, near the city of "Bampoora," about sixty miles from camp.

On 30th April, we all set out to beat a ravine about three miles off, named "Ramkoon," a very likely looking cover I had discovered when at this place last year, but no game was then found in it, most likely on account of the jungle being on fire all round. On arriving at the ground, we posted ourselves, two on either side of the deep ravine, remaining above, so as to command a view of the dense jungle below. Soon after the beaters had commenced making their usual noise, a large tiger was seen hastening out of the cover over the bare rocks below. He was directly fired at and hit hard. We now ran along the edge of the deep ravine on either side to keep him in view. Presently he stopped short under a thick bush. Here Little remained, keeping watch over him from above, while the rest of us returned to our original positions. Scarcely had we reached these and reloaded, when another tiger bolted out of the cover with loud roars. While we were busy firing at this one, out came two other tigers; these also got well "peppered" as they endeavoured to rush past us below, roaring terribly at our shots. We followed these brutes, as they made off, by running along the edge of the precipice, firing whenever a view of a tiger could be had as they rushed through the jungle beneath. Forbes and myself, who were both on the same side of this ravine, while thus running round a point at the entrance of the cover, saw from above a large bear walking quietly along in the plain below, having no doubt been disturbed by so much firing. We sent a few bullets at him also, but at so great a distance, that he could have been merely dusted by them as he strolled along a sandy path. The hint was enough for this bear, for he at once made off, at a racing pace, for another part of the hills.

We now all returned to the point from which the first

tiger was seen, to reload and fill our pouches with more bullets from the little bag of spare ammunition which each man always had carried with his spare guns. Here, to our great astonishment, yet another tiger was seen, slowly moving out of the cover directly below us. He was instantly riddled with bullets, but managed to hide himself quickly in some thick "corinda" bushes among the huge rocks that had fallen from the precipice above. By this time, the Bheels had finished beating this splendid cover; so we called some men, and placed them at certain points above on the look-out, while, with the rest of the men, we began the pleasant work of hunting up five wounded tigers that we knew were hiding in a space of about three hundred yards in the cover below. As usual, a procession was formed, and we proceeded most cautiously. Soon, a tiger was found lying dead at the mouth of a cave where he had crawled to hide himself. We passed on for about another fifty yards, when another tiger was also seen lying dead under a thick bush. We still continued the search, feeling far more comfortable, knowing that two of the enemy could lend no help in a general charge on our party, and had now reached the high broken mass of rocks and bushes where the big tiger had been last seen to lie up. We had carried on his track easily enough thus far, but could not discover it anywhere beyond. While we were prying about, and had even climbed on the top of these rocks to look out, a growl was heard, under our very feet it seemed. At the same moment Little discovered the old tiger lying in a cave formed of the large slabs of rock on which we were standing.

There was rather a hasty scramble out of this alarming neighbourhood; but Little, seeing how narrow the aperture was through which he had first viewed the tiger, at once began firing into the brute at only three yards' distance; in which work I also joined him, Forbes and Lock supplying us with spare loaded guns with admirable promptness from below. A further supply of these weapons the men quickly passed to the front. These we continued firing, as fast as they were handed up to us, at the tiger's head and shoulders, which was all that could be seen of him, until he ceased roaring, and was killed. On afterwards looking at this cave, we found this monster tiger had crept into it easily enough from an entrance in the rear, larger than the small one in front, from which he had so foolishly attempted to get out, whereby we became aware of his presence. Had he only chosen to emerge from the larger mouth of this den, he would have appeared right among us, and might have done much mischief, as we were not prepared for him.

We now tried for the other two wounded tigers; but could only take up their prints and blood for a short distance, owing to the dense jungle and rocky nature of the ground. These beasts, when last seen by us, were following each other out of this cover, going very slowly, and rolling and staggering along. It was now getting late, so we left off hunting for them any longer. My head man was at once sent to the nearest village to procure a bullock-cart, on which to carry home our game, while we returned to the ravine to collect the bodies of the slain, for there was not time enough to think of skinning them on the spot. We had much trouble in getting the dead tigers out of the different places where they had fallen; but at last, with the assistance of the men, we succeeded in placing all three brutes at the entrance of this ravine, near a rough sort of road. Very pretty they looked, lying side by side in a row, two tigers and a tigress. It now became quite dark; so, lighting a fire, we left twelve men in charge of the bodies, with three of our guns to protect them, in case the remaining wounded tigers should return to look for their murdered relatives, while we set out on our road home to the tents, three miles off, over most awfully stony ground. It was pitch dark, with very few stars to guide us, and our way lay through the cover out of which we had started so many tigers. Here large slippery rocks had to be scrambled over, and many falls and bruises occurred before we got clear of this dense mass of broken stones and jungle. It was half-past nine before we reached our little camp, all well tired and dreadfully thirsty.

We had given orders, before beating this ravine, for our horses to meet us in a few hours' time, thinking all the sport, if any, would be over by then. Our men brought the horses, but hearing the terrible row that was going on, and the extraordinary number of shots fired, while we were engaged with these five tigers and the bear, concluded something wrong was taking place; so they prudently returned with the horses out of danger.

To-day's ball-practice must have been very good, for the tigers seldom gave us a shot at less than fifty yards, mostly at double that distance. A tiger being but a very narrow animal, presents but a small mark when fired at from above. Besides, the exertion of running over broken ground, and loading at the same time, does not assist one's aim when firing at a brute making the best use of his legs to escape.

The three tigers arrived at our camp on the 1st May, on two carts, for the large tiger required a coach to himself, being so very heavy. It was thus late before the game reached us, on account of the great circuit, of at least twelve miles, round by the city of "Bampoora," which they had to make before they could reach the place where our tents were pitched. This had to be done, because there was no road of any sort across the way we had come home in the night.

Directly after breakfast we all set to work skinning the three tigers, by no means a pleasant job, for the game was already rather "high," after travelling so long in the sun. It always seemed to us somehow that tigers became sooner offensive after being shot than any other kind of animal, possibly from their living entirely on flesh. On killing a tiger, if we had reason to suppose another was still in the neighbourhood, before continuing to hunt down the living brute, we usually first carefully covered up the dead one with green branches, hastily cut down, or grass and reeds, collected for the purpose, so as to entirely protect the body from the sun. Or, if it had fallen on rocky ground, our first care was to remove the body under some shady bush, for if allowed to lie on the burning hot stones or rocks, even for a quarter of an hour or less, on raising it up, the hair on the side next the rocks would come off in flakes, whereby the skin was quite spoilt. It is almost impossible for those who have never experienced the heat, to conceive how terribly hot the rocks or stony ground exposed to the sun become during the "hot season;" so much so, that the hand cannot be kept on one particular spot for the space of even five seconds, without one's feeling glad enough to remove it. Precisely in the same manner our spare guns, if placed on the ground at our feet, exposed to the sun for even a few minutes, would become so dreadfully hot, that it was actually painful to handle the metal. For this purpose we were generally obliged to cover them with either green branches or waist-cloths, borrowed for a few minutes from the men who carried the spare guns. If obliged to either lie or sit down on these hot rocks, during the time the covers were being beaten, it was absolutely necessary to first spread over the burning ground some such protection as cloths or leaves, otherwise it would have been impossible to remain so perfectly still and quiet as is required to escape observation on these occasions.

At length we succeeeded in pegging down the three skins, when an extra dose of the arsenical soap was smeared over them to prevent any ill effects from their having already become so slightly tainted.

The rest of the day was devoted to cleaning and polishing

up our "battery," sorting and preparing ammunition, nailing on loose shoes of the horses, discussing oceans of that particularly agreeable drink called "mug," after our labours, taking frequent swims in the river, and other pleasant pastimes; for we could not think of hunting, as it was too late, after the tigers had been skinned, to set out to look for even the remaining two wounded tigers that escaped us on the previous evening. The men, too, had been up all night, keeping watch over the "game" collected at the entrance of "Ramkoon" ravine, waiting the arrival of the carts, and were too tired to be of any use; so all hands agreed to make holiday for once; moreover, it *happened* to be Sunday.

On the 2nd of May, we again beat "Ramkoon," stationing ourselves in a body below, this time; but nothing worth firing at appeared. We began hunting for the two wounded tigers, but could nowhere find them, although we made a long line, and searched for hours over an extensive patch of dense jungle in the plains, composed of long dry grass and thick thorn bushes, where the tigers were last seen. The following day also proved blank. We merely saw some herds of cheetul deer, but did not fire. Our tents were now at Gole Ambah village, eight miles distant.

Having tried over the most likely ground near this village, but without success, we agreed to have a day's "sambur" shooting, for the sake of the leather, of which article we stood in much need to make new shooting-shoes. The sambur at this place were very numerous, so we arranged to hunt from here to "Goola" village, eight miles off, over some famous ground covered with a dense jungle of thorn bushes, high grass, large broken rocks, and clumps of low shady trees, under which herds of cheetul and sambur reposed during the heat of the day. Not expecting to find any "large game," for the previous day we had been unable to discover even prints of it anywhere about in the covers we had beaten, it was settled that we should separate at intervals of about two hundred yards, and hunt parallel to each other over this likely country, as far as the river "Chumbul," about seven miles off; then to assemble there and compare notes of our sport. Each hunter, accompanied by two Bheels to carry his spare guns and water-bag, at once spread themselves in a line. Little and Lock remained on the top of a low range of hills on the right, the sides of which were almost perpendicular walls of rock, while Forbes took the outside or extreme left point; the centre was my beat.

We had advanced for about a mile, occasionally firing at deer as they were started in front of us, when suddenly a loud roar was heard; and a fine tiger was seen, by those above on the edge of the rocky hills, to bound out of some caves immediately below them. Little and Lock directly fired four rifle-shots at the beast, as he made off in the plain below, and then loudly called to me to "look out." I also had heard this roaring plainly enough, but at the time concluded it was only an old bear that had been fired at, for I was unable to see above a few score yards at most around me, on account of the dense jungle. Almost directly afterwards, I caught a glimpse of the tiger, as it came crashing through and bounding over the thick bushes, at a great pace, straight down towards where I was standing with my two Bheels. It was roaring fearfully as it came on, tail up and claws out. There was but time to whisper the men with me to be quite still and silent, when the tiger passed, about ten yards only in my front, at full gallop. I waited until it had just got by, and then fired, rolling the beast over with the first ball. It quickly jumped up, and turned round, looking full at me; but another shot somewhere about the face or neck made it once more rush forward on its course.

Forbes, who was about a hundred yards off on my left, now called out to know what I was firing at. On hearing his voice, the tiger at once turned off to the front, with extra roars, fortunately enough, or in another second or two, he also would have had a close meeting with this beauty; and, being even less prepared than I was, might have met with some damage from the enraged beast. The two men with me behaved admirably; neither spoke or moved an inch, although we were standing on almost perfectly level ground, and the tiger appeared to be coming as direct as possible towards where we standing. Little and Lock, from above, could plainly see all that passed, and continued to loudly warn me of my danger. They wondered at first why I had allowed the tiger to go by without firing, as it came charging down towards me; and fancied I was unable to see it clear enough on account of the thick jungle. But they cheered on seeing it drop.

We now all joined each other below, and in a body, with the few men we had with us, began carefully following up the prints of this wounded tiger. We had much difficulty in doing this, for the ground was very stony. However, we saw, in two or three places, where this brute had fallen down and dragged itself over the rough stones, leaving tufts of hair on the sharp rocks and bushes around. Every moment we expected to put him up, or find the tiger dead; but, as ill luck would have it, the blood soon entirely ceased, and we were unable to carry on the prints any further over such stony ground. The men now thought, from the direction in which this wounded tiger appeared to be going, that he must be making straight for some water a little way off. We at once went there, as this suggestion seemed probable enough. On reaching this pool of water, a cowherd, who was tending a drove of bullocks near at hand, came running up to us to say that a tiger had just killed one of his cows in an open field close by, and offered to point out the place he had gone to lie up in. We at once accompanied this man, and saw the dead cow just killed and untouched; but, after beating among a number of high rocks, and looking over innumerable caves around, we were unable to find this second tiger.

It was now too late to attempt hunting for the first wounded one any longer, so we walked over to our tents along the banks of the river "Chumbul," finding many alligator's, or perhaps the large freshwater turtle's, eggs, on our way. These were white, soft, nearly round, pulpy-looking balls, strung together like snake's eggs, about the size of a duck's egg. Many seemed to have been dug up out of the sand on the river's banks, and been eaten by the numerous mongooses or ichneumons about. We did not reach our tents till dark, rather vexed at so losing to-day's tiger; but it could not be helped; and, seeing how utterly unprepared we were to meet such a brute, it was not much to be wondered at that he escaped us. On the contrary, we rather had cause to rejoice that we escaped him. It serves to prove the necessity of being always together, and at all times ready for the fiercest beast that may appear, while hunting for merely deer even. Had the brave fellows with me to-day made the slightest attempt at escape, instead of remaining perfectly still, as directed, this tiger would certainly have noticed, and as surely charged us. As it was, thanks to our dark clothes, he never saw us until too late to do much mischief.

On the 5th May, we beat several very likely covers about "Goola" village, and along the river "Chumbul," even beyond "Shamghur" fort, but no game was seen, although plenty of fresh prints were found. At midnight, while, as usual, sleeping out, for coolness sake, in the open air, an awful row was suddenly heard in the midst of our encampment. Everybody instantly turned out to ascertain the cause of the disturbance. We soon discovered that a panther had paid us a visit, and, after killing a goat in the very midst of our servants and tents, had the audacity to carry off my two large greyhounds, named "Goldie" and "Bessie." These dogs were coupled together, and tied to a tent-peg at the side of my cot. The panther dragged both these dogs for about three hundred yards over and through some terribly dense jungle of high thorn-bushes. Guided by the bitch's loud cries and barking, we followed as quickly as possible, firing off guns, shouting, and waving lighted brands, snatched from the fires around. Soon we came upon the spot where the panther had at last dropped these dogs, which he did on our nearing him while thus giving chase. The poor dog "Goldie" was killed, his skull having been smashed in by a blow of the panther's paw; but the bitch "Bessie" was all right, except the fright she had received. While thus hastening to the rescue, I got severely scratched and bruised by tumbling over thorn-bushes and large stones; for the night was very dark, and I had merely my shirt and slippers on at the time. Finding he could not carry off the goat, which was firmly tied up for the night, this panther had made a snatch at my dogs, and succeeded in uprooting the tent-peg to which they, for safety sake, were always fastened at night. No doubt he would have been satisfied with one, but was compelled to take both hounds, on account of their being linked together.

To give some idea of the panther's strength, I may state that these greyhounds had, on more than one occasion, successfully encountered even full-grown wolves. Panthers are much in the habit of preying upon unfortunate "pariahs," or common dogs, without any particular owners, that swarm at every village throughout India. These unlucky curs, according to the Bheels' account, the panther easily catches, by making an unusual noise on any dark night near the walls of the village. On hearing the noise, out rush the dogs with loud barking. The foremost is pretty sure to be pounced upon and carried off by the lurking panther. These brutes are very bold and cunning. Being well able to see in the dark, this panther had not hesitated to walk among our servants while they were sleeping on the ground, and kill the poor goat that was picketed in the middle of the men, lying close together. It moved about so stealthily that it failed to even disturb my dogs until they were also seized.

Early next morning, after erecting a pile of large stones over the greyhound's grave, we started to hunt up this panther, visiting every likely place in which he was supposed to live, but without being able to discover the brute.

While at breakfast, two Bheels came to tell us that they had last night shot a tiger, while lying in wait by moonlight over a small pool of water, expecting sambur, hog, and cheetul, to come down to drink. Returning homewards, they came upon the tiger quite dead, having been shot through the liver by a very small matchlock bullet. The liver affords a capital mark to fire at in a tiger, for such a wound is always fatal within a few minutes, for the animal quickly bleeds to death internally, or is choked with blood; but, for the time being, it does not in the slightest degree disable the tiger.

CHAPTER XVIII.

SUCCESSFUL TACTICS—A DAY'S BATTLING—TWO TIGERS SLAIN—A TROUBLESOME CUSTOMER—THE HUNTERS HUNTED—A HARD-LIVED BEAST—KILLED AT LAST.

HUNTING onward to the village of Booj, we were told of a very large tiger that lived in the beautiful willow-bush covers in the bed of the river there. This tiger was said to have only lately come to reside in the neighbourhood, yet he had already killed thirteen large buffaloes, and some cows. From this we knew he must be a full-grown male. We tried about two miles of the covers along the river, but without success. On the next day, we renewed our search, and tried several small patches of thick jungle, near the village in which he was said to be often seen, but without being able to find him at home in any of them. We then went ahead, intending to have a very long drive for this beast among the dense willow-bushes far up the stream. Presently, Little saw the tiger moving off about a hundred yards in front, along the very path we were walking. We quickly now ran on the outside of the cover for about four hundred yards, making a circuit, in the hope of being able to get ahead of this tiger, for he was moving very slowly. We stopped short over a small ravine branching out of the big river covers. Here we soon after saw the tiger quite close, going up a small bank before us; we fired a few shots, on which the tiger roared and immediately bolted off out of sight. We were not quite prepared at the time; for, oddly enough, directly before this tiger appeared, in the very same spot two "beadlahs," or ravine deer, had jumped up out of the long grass; so some of us fancied for the moment that, instead of the tiger, the animal in front was merely another deer. We now again went round outside the cover in the same manner, to head the tiger for about half a mile. While waiting here, a bear and two sambur came close by us, but were not fired at, as we expected better game. When the beaters joined us we directed them to be silent for a short time, while we once more went ahead, outside the river covers, for nearly two miles, at the very end almost of the ravine. There we took up our position on the edge of a high rocky bank, and were presently delighted to hear the monkeys loudly swearing in all directions which signal gave warning of the tiger's approach. We saw him coming straight for our post from a long distance, and allowed him to nearly pass us about thirty yards off in the cover below, when a volley was poured in, which caused the tiger to instantly rear bolt upright and dance about on his hind legs, striking wildly all round him with his fore-paws, at the same time uttering frightful roars. On a sudden he attempted to rush back through the dense cover, but a further dose of lead stopped him. We now left our position, and went down to look at the enemy; as he still showed slight signs of life, a few more bullets were administered, when all was still. We skinned the tiger on the spot, in some little dread of the numerous bees' nests around, for these insects are apt to be disturbed on any strange smell or noise. By good luck, they did not turn out on our firing at this beast, for we afterwards found out that we had been sitting immediately over several nests of them. Got home by dusk after a four-mile walk back, and pegged down the skin, which was a very handsome one. Returning, I shot a "murrel" fish, two-and-a-half feet long, for dinner.

For the next eight days we unluckily met with no large game, although hunting daily over the best part of the country for sport we knew. By this time, after several marches, we had reached "Limree" again. Here, early on the morning of 16th May, a cowherd came running to our camp to tell us that a tiger had just killed one of his oxen while they were grazing, near a very thick cover of high thorn-bushes and brushwood, on the side of a long low hill. We at once set out for the spot, but on arriving there, were annoyed to find that several tanners, or leather sellers, had already begun skinning the dead bullock, having also heard of the "kill." These men stated that, by making a great noise, they had driven off two tigers that were lurking in the neighbouring thicket. We beat a few patches of thick jungle close by, but without seeing anything; and were about to return to breakfast, when a woodcutter called after us and said that he had just seen the two tigers pass by where he was at work felling trees, about a mile distant. Hearing the noise of our drums and pistols, he at once ran to tell us what he had seen. It was now too cool and early in the morning, so we agreed to let the tigers alone until the day became hotter, when we should have a better chance of finding them in some cover where they would be sure to lie up during the heat of the day; whereas, if we hunted them then, they would make off miles away. We returned home and again started at half-past eleven A.M., to beat the cover on this long sloping bank or rising ground. Little and Lock remained at the foot of a small hill, while Forbes and I stood exactly opposite them, on the top, overlooking the cover. Soon after the beating commenced, I saw a tiger moving very cautiously just in front of the men, who, as usually happened, were quite unaware of her presence. She came within about forty yards of where our comrades were posted, and then stopped still to look at them. Whereupon, Lock and myself both fired a shot each, and well knew she was hit. The tiger instantly bolted back towards the men, who quickly sprang up the surrounding trees on hearing the firing and roaring in front. Forbes also got a shot as she rushed back, but Little unluckily never saw her until too late. We now all four joined the beaters, and with them began following up the blood and prints. After going a short distance this tigress was found dead under a bush. I happened to look round and then saw two young tigers—mere cubs, about twenty inches high—pass close by where Forbes and self were sitting.

I fired, but did not drop either of these "kittens." We then walked forward, each taking merely a double rifle for the chance of again meeting these young tigers, leaving the rest of our guns with the beaters, whom we directed to follow us making a noise. For such cubs we considered ourselves quite sufficiently armed, and were very careless as to where we stood. After going on about five hundred yards, Little and Lock both sat down on a low stone. Forbes got into a small tree to look out over the cover, while I stood on a higher piece of rock to guard the ground in the rear. Almost directly after the beating again began, Forbes, to his great surprise, saw a magnificent tiger walk by close under his tree; he fired, and the brute bounded off roaring; but, on Forbes giving him another shot, he changed his course, and came rushing on within six or eight paces of where Little and Lock were sitting. They were on a perfect level with this enraged tiger. Little instantly gave him a shot in the face, which fortunately dropped him; and there the beast lay for some little time groaning; but on receiving Little's second barrel, jumped up, and with terrible roars at once bolted back with long bounds towards where the men were advancing. I now got a running shot at about eighty paces, and luckily broke the tiger's fore-arm, which at once stopped him when within a very short distance only of the beaters; who, thinking we were merely polishing off the cubs, were much scattered about, and were carelessly walking through the jungle, without preserving their usual compact formation. Lock all this time had kept guard with his rifle as a reserve to Little's shots. The men, hearing the roars so near them, at once sprang up trees, where they remained safe until we again joined them, when we all advanced together towards where the tiger had pulled up, taking good care this time to have our spare guns behind us. The tiger was hiding in a small patch of very thick jungle, composed of large broken pieces of rock, high grass, and dense thorn-bushes. He would not show, but growled awfully. No doubt he was too much crippled to charge. We went up within fifteen paces of this thicket, and fired in some shots at random. At length he once more attempted to bolt from the rear of this patch of jungle, but was quickly rolled over. On giving him more shots, he again recovered his legs, and once more tried to break back but was floored again. His efforts to escape, while going off through the high grass, gave us opportunities of finally knocking him over. On cautiously approaching, we found this tiger lying flat on his side quite dead in the high grass. He was a very fine stout tiger, in his prime, and measured eleven feet ten inches long.

This was altogether a very lucky escape for most of our hunting party, especially Little and Lock, who were directly in the tiger's path, and consequently stood a most ugly chance of being charged when first met by this wounded tiger. It served to show the necessity for being at all times most fully armed and prepared for the largest even while looking for the smallest of tigers.

We never again saw the cubs. A camel was sent for from our tents, while we, with much bother, conveyed the bodies of these two tigers clear of the thick jungle through which we were obliged to cut a path with axes before they could be got outside this cover. Did not return till quite dark to our encampment. The cattle-owners here were particularly delighted with our success.

For the following three days we looked in vain over many covers, but found no sport. A good deal of rain fell during this time. The baggage, by easy stages, had been moved on from "Limree" to the large village of "Oomurchee," above the range of hills. On our road here we heard that a Bheel of this place had the day before fired at a large tiger from a tree, on its coming down to eat a bullock it had previously killed. After looking over a few likely places, but without success, we began beating a small rocky ravine close to the village. The men had hardly commenced their uproar, when we saw a large tiger crawl out of a cave, about a hundred yards lower down the cover over which we were keeping watch. Having previously hunted over this ground, I was able to guess the direction in which the tiger would most likely make off; for, on getting out of the cave, it at once had left the cover altogether, and had gone in quite another track to what we expected. Hastily snatching up our spare guns, we at once ran off as fast as possible for about a quarter of a mile towards a low bank overlooking another small, but extremely thick, patch of jungle. Scarcely had we climbed up some very slight and ricketty trees near this cover, which was the only means we had of overlooking the grass around, when we saw the tiger galloping towards our position. He passed within about fifty yards straight for the very cover we were guarding. I alone was able to get two clear shots at him, both of which hit. Little and Loch also made the tiger growl as they fired, but at an awkward distance. Forbes was altogether out of the line of fire, so could not shoot. The men soon afterwards joined us. We tried hard with them to take up the tiger's blood, but could nowhere find any, greatly to our surprise. After, with much difficulty, following up the prints, for the ground was terribly stony, we left the beaters; and, each taking two guns, went silently round to the opposite end of the small but dense ravine towards which the tiger had gone off. This little cover was formed of corinda bushes, green reeds, high grass, clumps of bamboo, and thorn bushes, closely mingled. The beating noise was resumed, and the dry grass set on fire. Almost immediately afterwards, Forbes saw the tiger quietly creeping past a tree, up which he and I had climbed on the edge of the low ravine. Forbes fired, and rolled over the tiger; but, on giving him another shot, the beast jumped up, and bolted back into the dense jungle again. I was not able or ready to fire. Neither could Little or Loch fire from the position they had chosen, although they saw the tiger creeping out of this small ravine even before we did. The men continued beating, and soon afterwards Little saw the tiger making across an open plain for the very cover out of which we had first started him. He fired one shot, which the tiger acknowledged with a growl, but the distance was too great to do much harm. We now again all together tried to take up the prints; but the ground here being very stony, or, for the most part, mere "sheet" rock resembling pavement, these could not be carried on far; while, still, to our great astonishment, not even a drop of blood could anywhere be seen.

On arriving at the cover we had first of all beaten, we left the Bheels behind with orders to recommence beating this ravine in a different direction, while we each, taking two rifles, went ahead to take up a fresh position. Making a circuit of about three hundred yards, we, as quietly as possible, approached the edge of the ravine, with the view of selecting some good commanding point over the cover below, and were standing on a low sloping bank, when suddenly the tiger jumped up at our very feet, out of some high grass in which he had been lying down, and with loud roars bounded off towards the opposite bank of the ravine. No doubt the surprise of thus again so unexpectedly meeting each other was mutual; but we fired sharply several shots as the tiger made off, and at last saw him enter a dense patch of jungle on the opposite sloping bank of this ravine. Just as we had reloaded, the men began beating, when we saw this tiger stealthily trying to escape out of the cover in which he had last sought refuge by crawling over the bank opposite our post, about eighty yards off. We once more gave him the contents of our "battery;" when the brute rushed forward for a few paces, but then suddenly turned round, and came charging down with fearful roars straight for where we were standing. All the guns being *empty*, it was now our turn to bolt. Little, Loch, and Forbes, with wonderful agility, sprang up three small trees that happened to be close behind us. For the moment, I could nowhere find a tree; and, in my hurry and confusion, ran down a gentle slope of the bank on which we had been standing, and dived under a shady bush at the bottom of the low hill, out of which I started a hare. Here I remained perfectly still, in the utmost alarm; for, in the panic, I had chosen the most likely spot by which the tiger would pass as he tried to escape us. This dreadful thought only occurred to me while lying under the bush in which I endeavoured to conceal myself. Every moment I expected to see the tiger go by, but most fortunately he pulled up in his charge under the trees up which my three friends had sought safety. Here he continued for some time walking round and round the trees, looking up at his enemies, growling terribly, and lashing his tail in a great rage. Luckily he was too much hurt to make a spring. Little treated him rather contemptuously from his secure position, and declared that with a pistol even he could easily have blown out the tiger's brains as he passed so close below his tree. At length the tiger slowly took himself off, and walked back to the very dense patch of jungle out of which he had last broken before we had thus caused him to charge. All this time my friends had repeatedly called out to me, not knowing where I was hiding; but I did not dare answer, for fear the tiger should discover my retreat, when, being utterly unarmed, with the exception of my heavy hunting-knife, there would have been no chance even of escape for me. At last they bawled out that the tiger had gone away, when I joyfully emerged from the thorn-bush, and hastily reloaded my rifle, feeling once more secure.

We now all went towards the beaters, and again tried to start this tiger, but could not again make him show himself, though men were sent up very high trees overlooking the thick cover in which he was hiding. It was now getting late, so we reluctantly left the place, hoping to find this tiger dead there on the morrow.

Wonderful to relate, when last seen he seemed as fresh as the moment we first started him, and appeared actually invulnerable, for not one drop of his blood could we anywhere discover, although, on afterwards counting over our ammunition, we computed that forty-two bullets (including some guns double-shotted) had been fired at this tiger. None of us had ever before met with such a beast seemingly so bullet-proof. We returned to our tents by dusk, much perplexed at the day's work, having been fairly beaten by this tiger.

Next morning, 21st May, we again visited the thicket in which we had last evening left the tiger, and walked most carefully through the whole cover, but still, strange to say, could find no blood. We next, by chance, intending to hunt for him from a cover some distance off, passed by the small ravine where the men had set fire to the high grass. Here we came upon the tiger's fresh prints, and, following them, soon found plenty of blood. We took these prints easily as far as a ravine named "Neereea Kal," about two miles off, and beat this long cover in two drives, but no tiger appeared. We then agreed to go back through this ravine and carefully examine every part of it, expecting to find this tiger dead. We had gone thus through the thickest part of the cover, when suddenly one of my men and myself saw the tiger lying down close in front of us, apparently dead.

At this time we were rather scattered and walking carelessly over what seemed not the most likely spot to find the

Lieut. W. Rice Del.

tiger in. Little was gathering "corinda" berries to eat, while Forbes, before being aware of his danger, strolled on within four yards of the tiger, when the brute's ear was observed to move. The alarm was quickly, but silently, given to the rest of our men following behind us. With all the guns and beaters we climbed up a steep bank overlooking the thicket in which the tiger was hiding, and then fired a volley into him quite close, from some high rocks on which we were standing directly over the beast. Up jumped the tiger, and with loud roars he endeavoured to get out of the small cover; but was quickly rolled over for good by our guns. This brute still seemed quite fresh and active, although, on skinning him, which we at once proceeded to do, no less than twelve of yesterday's bullets were found in his body. These we knew by the marks he had made in licking them with his tongue, clearing off the hair round each shot-hole. A tiger's tongue is remarkably rough and covered with innumerable stout short points of hard flesh, resembling thorns, closely packed together, and lying backwards. With these he easily scrapes off every atom of flesh adhering to the bones of his prey.

This tiger measured eleven feet six inches long, and was extremely stout. At the time we found him, he was lying with his body half in some water to allay the pain of his wounds. Over head was a beautiful "oleander" bush in full blossom. These pretty pink and white flowers are very common in all the jungles about this part of the country. Forbes had rather a narrow escape, had he not been warned in time by my man, of stepping on this crouching tiger.

CHAPTER XIX.

DACOITS—HOW THEY DEAL WITH THEIR WOUNDED—MY COMRADES QUIT ME—A TOUGH BEAR—AN AGREEABLE SURPRISE—FALL LAME, BUT HUNT STILL—SURPRISED AND KILLED—A NOCTURNAL VISITOR—DISAPPOINTED—FACE TO FACE—THE LAST SHOT—THE BAG.

WELL satisfied with our sport in the "Oomurchee" ravine, we moved on to "Koree" village on the following morning, but for two days found nothing worth a shot.

But on 24th May, having arrived at "Ruttenghur" fort, where a great fair was being held, we proceeded to beat "Inhadeo Kullah," about two miles off. Here we discovered the fresh prints of an enormous tiger, and soon aftewards found that he had killed and half eaten a camel very lately. This again raised our spirits. The ravine there is very steep, and rather wide; so, to guard all parts of it, Little and Loch agreed to remain below, getting up into a small shady tree to hide themselves, while Forbes and I climbed up one side of the steep hill, and posted ourselves on a rocky ledge above, overlooking the cover, and opposite a small ruined fort on the other bank. The men were sent round to the far end of the cover to beat; scarcely had they commenced making their usual noise and firing a few shots, when, to our wonder, a terrific uproar arose among them. They at once began running off in all directions at their utmost speed, throwing down the drums, bell, and other instruments, in their flight. What most puzzled us was hearing more shots than they had pistols fired at the time. At first Forbes and I concluded that the tiger might have broke cover over the steep hill among the beaters, but this was very improbable, and then that the confounded bees might have attacked them, so we remained perfectly quiet. Soon a man passed by where we were lying down, calling out loudly that thieves were killing our people. We at once jumped up, and each taking a double rifle, ran towards the place pointed out. Here we saw about a dozen men or more near the small ruined fort across the ravine. Three or four of these fellows had matchlocks, while the rest were armed only with swords or bows and arrows. Nearly every man had a large bundle, with which he was laden. They had fired a shot at our beaters just as we came up, so we loudly called to them to put down their guns and stop firing. One of them now advanced to the edge of the deep ravine between us, knelt down, placed his matchlock between the forked branches of a low tree as a rest, took a long deliberate aim at Forbes and myself as we stood together calling to the men to disperse, and to our astonishment fired, for we fancied he merely intended to frighten us away. We directly replied, with one shot each in return, and great was the noise and howling that ensued. At the same time the thieves quickly ran off into the ruined fort. We fired a few other shots well over their heads, when they at once disappeared.

The probability is that the man who fired at us was hit, but we never went to look as we had another cover to beat close by. He was about eighty to a hundred yards off. Our men much wished us to polish off these rogues, but as none of our followers had been shot—merely frightened—we did not like to fire on the rascals. These thieves no doubt thought we had come to attack them, not knowing that we were merely hunting for a tiger.

All this time Little and Loch, perched in a tree below, were much puzzled by what was going on above, for they could see nothing from their position. They only heard the firing and shouting. We afterwards heard that many people attending this large fair at "Ruttenghur" had been robbed on the roads.

The thieves had no doubt driven away the tiger we were after from this ravine, in which they also were hiding, for we tried several other covers about, but could nowhere find the beast. Just before leaving the place, we saw a high column of black smoke arise from the ruined fort. This our men thought might be caused by the robbers burning the body of their wounded companion; for these fellows, they assured us, if in dread of pursuit, seldom impeded their flight by carrying off any of their number who might be badly wounded, but at once put them out of all pain; and to efface any traces that might lead to detection, or the capture of the gang, quickly covered them with dry grass, pouring over the heap plenty of oil, and set fire to the whole, leaving nothing behind by which they might be discovered.

On returning to our tents, we reported the circumstance to the native police at "Ruttenghur" fort. These men at once went after the rogues, but could not discover them.

Next day Little, Forbes, and Loch, rode back to camp, their leave of absence having expired; so I moved on to "Doraee" village to hunt alone as long as my leave lasted. Here I got a shot at a panther going up a steep hill covered with thorn-bushes; but fancy my bullet must have missed, although only about forty paces off, for we could find no blood. At night a perfect hurricane came on, with much rain. My small tent was blown down.

On the 27th, while beating "Bunsur" ravine, I wounded a bear, but he got off. I then moved my baggage on to "Jaat," and set off to beat a ravine among the hills behind "Sanda" village. Here a bear turned out, at which I fired very unwillingly, for I expected nobler game. My shot brought the bear down the steep hill, rolling over and over like a large round rock. I gave him another bullet on reaching the bottom at

about fifteen yards off, and as he moaned much, concluded he was dying. No other animal appeared, so I turned to look for the bear, but he had somehow disappeared without my knowledge. While walking up a hill close by, I suddenly came upon this bear, trying to hide himself behind a large tree. I got within thirty yards, and gave him both barrels of my rifle, when off he started again, seemingly as fresh as ever. It was not worth while pursuing him, so I walked over the hills straight for "Sanda" village. Here, strange enough, I again put up this bear quite close, and again wounded him; when last seen, the brute was making off in quite a contrary direction. A man now climbed a high tree, and said he could see the bear going very slowly a little distance in front through some very thick thorn-bushes, so I ran forward and overtook the bear, killing him close to the village, where we skinned him under a shady tree. Oddly enough, he showed no signs of being wounded, but was really riddled with bullets

On the road past "Lohareea" cover, I heard that a large tiger was said to live there, having lately killed several bullocks close by. I at once determined to beat the cover, although it was nearly five o'clock in the evening, and quite cool, which gave but a poor chance of seeing game. The men quickly began beating, while I stationed myself on a bank near one end of the jungle. Almost instantly, a magnificent tiger passed about twenty yards in my front; I fired at his head, whereupon the tiger reared bolt upright in the air; but my second ball caused him to spring forward, with terrible roars, into another patch of willow bushes just beyond. On my men coming up they agreed to go round, and try once more to start this tiger. Warning them to keep well clear of the cover, they began again making a noise, when, with much crashing of bushes, the tiger repassed my post at a gallop across a small open space. Here he received one ball in the shoulders and another in the chest as he raced by. Another shot told somewhere about his ribs as he disappeared in a long bound into the dense jungle out of which he had been first started. It was now just sunset, so I did not attempt to follow up the blood, quantities of which we discovered before leaving this cover.

At night, another edition of the hurricane, with much lightning.

On the 29th May, having selected some good men, I started to hunt up yesterday's wounded tiger. I must own to somehow feeling very unwilling for this work, for the cover was terribly thick. We could not see even three yards ahead. Moreover, the thoughts of the last tiger killed at "Oomurchee," that had so bothered even four of us, forced themselves on my mind, but there was no help for it. Keeping an extra bright look-out, the procession was formed; when, after most cautiously advancing about fifty yards only into the thick jungle, to my great joy the tiger was seen lying dead just before us. He was a very fine beast indeed—measured eleven feet eight inches long. We skinned him on the spot, and then returned to Jaat to peg down the skin. My first shot had passed clean through both the tiger's cheeks; this caused him to rear so.

For the next five days I got no sport, although I moved on to "Panghur." A panther was heard roaring all night, but it seemed impossible to find him. At this place I became very lame from falling over a stone, that caused my foot to swell dreadfully. The weather was very cool now, with frequent showers of rain. Here I again heard a cuckoo very plain.

On the 4th of June, I started to beat "Barodeo" cover, three miles off. Seating myself on the rocky ledge of one side of this ravine, a fine tiger soon turned out and came slowly on right under me, not ten yards off; but here I could not fire at his head, on account of a thick bush covering him, under which he stopped for a short time to listen to the beaters behind. On his again moving on, I fired away as sharply as possible.

The guns, from lying on this bare rock so long in the sun, were so dreadfully hot, that I could barely hold them. The tiger never spoke, but rushed forward over an open hill close by, leaving the cover altogether. On the men coming up, we began following up his blood.

Soon, a man placed to look out up a tree discovered the tiger dead a short distance beyond where I had last seen him bounding off over the little hill. We skinned him on the spot. This tiger was a fine stout beast, measuring eleven feet ten inches long. Being still lame, the pace, while following up to-day, was a very cautious one indeed.

On my way to "Gatowlee" village, the next day, we saw a bear walking about on a steep hill-side, though it was now just mid-day, a clear proof of the coolness of the weather. After watching him for some time with my small telescope, I saw this bear lie up under a shady tree, where he remained for a long while without moving off. Taking two Bheels with me to carry the spare guns, I explained to the rest of my men how they should direct me to the spot from the opposite hill-side, while advancing towards this bear, by waving their turbans and other private signals. By these means I managed to get within twelve yards of the bear, walking on tiptoe to the exact spot where he was lying, when up he got; but was almost directly shot dead. Rolling the body down to the bottom of the steep hill, it was carried on to "Gatowlee" village, by some of the men close by, to await my coming there. Another bear was started out of some caves near the hill, but he got out at too great a distance to make sure of hitting him. I fired one shot as he bolted off into some extremely dense jungle, where he was lost to sight. We now all together walked across an open plain, about two miles, to another range of hills opposite. I climbed up to the top of these steep hills, taking two Bheels with me to carry the spare guns and water-bag. The rest remained below, with orders to commence beating the thick jungle on this hill-side, as soon as sufficient time had elapsed to allow of my taking up a position some good distance beyond on the summit of the hill.

While thus walking along the top and occasionally looking over the precipice at the jungle below, I saw a tigress lying in the shade of a small tree, stretched out on a large rock about fifteen paces below, just outside a deep cave directly under where I was standing. She seemed utterly unaware of my presence, for the Bheels and self had, as usual, been walking as silently as possible. I fired one shot sharp at her head, and luckily killed this tigress dead. She neither spoke nor even moved, except to stretch herself out with a quivering movement. The men, who had never heard this shot, began now to beat this hill-side, but no more game appeared. She measured 9 feet 10½ inches long, and under her jacket we discovered three matchlock bullets; so some natives had evidently hunted her before. Returned home by sunset, and pegged down both the bear's and tigress' skins.

At night we were disturbed by hearing a large tiger roaring quite close to the tent. There was no moon at the time, so he could not be seen. He remained some time, repeating the roaring at intervals, to the great alarm of my horses and servants. I turned out in my shirt all ready, but could see nothing, although the noise seemed only about thirty or forty paces off. It was no use firing at hazard. The tent was pitched close to a small lake at which this tiger was in the habit of drinking at night, for his prints there were numerous enough, and perhaps our presence disturbed him. I felt certain of being able to kill this tiger next morning, but after beating all day long over many large hills could nowhere find him. At one steep hill a bear turned out, and passed close by my post. I rolled him over, and broke his fore arm, but he escaped; for we did not attempt to follow up his blood, of which a good quantity had been spilt. Many wild boars, with their families, came down to drink at the lake in the evening, but I did not fire at the pork. Next day again tried the hills around for the big tiger, but only saw some sambur, at which I did not fire.

Moved the baggage on to "Sumilpoora," a village six miles further north, close to the large hill-fort of "Chittore," a noted stronghold of the "Rajpoot" princes in former days, but now in ruins. I hunted for the next four days in this neighbourhood, but without success. At one place a fine panther was started, but out of shot unluckily. At another cover, in which prints of a large tiger were found, quite fresh after drawing, the place blank. I saw a peacock, of which birds, as usual, swarms were roused, on attempting to settle under a large solitary "corinda" bush in an open space, fly off again in a great state of alarm uttering its loud warning note of danger; so concluded that the tiger must be hid in that very bush. Collecting the men, we cautiously and silently walked up within about twenty yards of the bush, into which a volley of stones was flung; but, greatly to my disappointment, only three red "pariahs," or common dogs, ran out yelping towards their village, about a mile off. These curs had been lying in the shade of this thick bush for the coolness. The men much laughed at this finish to the precautions I had taken of keeping them well together and silent.

On the 12th June, having by this time arrived at "Paal" village, near the large town of "Bussee," while looking over some hills covered with dense brushwood, I suddenly came upon a panther, not quite full grown, and rolled him over dead with two shots of my rifle. Leaving him under a shady rock, I went about a quarter of a mile ahead, directing the men to beat a steep hill covered with jungle towards my position, which was on the edge of a steep rocky bank. Two men that were returning to the rest of the beaters, after leaving me with my guns at this point, met a tiger walking over an open space between two hills. They quickly climbed up some high trees, and from these watched the tiger enter another patch of jungle some little distance beyond. Then, descending, they ran to the beaters, and warned them of what they had seen. These men very properly went round, and at once began beating the thicket in which the tiger was hiding, driving him in my direction. It seemed strange to me to hear the men making a noise in this unexpected quarter, but soon after I saw a tiger quietly walking straight for the place where I was lying down. My guns were all turned the wrong way, for I was looking out in a contrary direction. The tiger came on slowly within twenty paces, when she stopped and stared hard at me for about two minutes; I remained perfectly still, when, to my delight, the tiger moved on, turning off a little to one side down a sloping bank. Directly the last tip of its tail had disappeared I raised myself up until a fair view of the retreating tiger could be had, when I shot her dead with the first ball. She made a tremendous leap forward in the air, when I again fired; but, being much excited, this shot missed altogether. The tiger fell to the ground without even a groan or kick. When the Bheels joined me, we skinned this tigress on the spot; she measured ten feet six inches, and was stout. Some men were sent to carry home the dead panther to my tent. Both skins were pegged down by sunset.

This tigress served me much the same trick as did one at "Panghur," on 13th June, 1852. I was lying flat on some rocks of a reddish tint much resembling the colour of my clothes. The guns were covered with green boughs. No doubt she mistook me for a mere stone. The suspense while she moved her head backwards and forwards as she peered at me was awful, but it was useless to move, as she could have

LAST TIGER SEEN

charged long before I could have got a gun ready to bear on her. The shots at the panther had most likely disturbed her, when so luckily seen by the two Bheels.

This was the last shot I had this "season" at large game, for the "monsoon," or rainy season, now set in with such violence that it was useless attempting to hunt any longer, although a few days of my leave yet remained. Being rather more than forty miles to camp, I started homewards at once, for the ground was so muddy and slippery from the heavy rains that the camels with difficulty could only march a few miles each day. For about four days we were wet through, day and night. It rained incessantly, so there was no opportunity of drying anything, either by the sun or fires. At night, mostly, fearful hurricanes came on, so that the country was strewed with uprooted trees, and large branches blown down. On 18th June, the last day of my leave, I reached "Tarrapoor," eleven miles from camp. The river there, which in the hot weather is generally nearly dry, was now a boiling torrent, on account of the heavy rains and numerous streams that flowed from the hills into it, about a hundred yards or more across. Fearing that the river might increase in width and violence if more rain fell, by which I should be detained some days perhaps, before being able to cross at all (as on a former occasion once happened to a party of three of us), I at once determined to swim across this river. A Bheel, with my pony and saddle, on which my clothes were bound, went first; they landed at least four hundred yards down the stream, being carried away by the rapid current. The pony, on reaching the shore, was so done that he lay down there and then. Placing my watch and pistol in the folds of my turban bound round my hunting cap, I swam over safe but was taken down quite as far as the Bheel and pony had been. Luckily the rain now ceased, and by night this violent river had so subsided that the camels easily crossed over. Had the storms continued, they would have been stopped for a week perhaps, as there is no bridge of any sort over this stream.

The "bag," this trip, which might have been larger had the weather been rather warmer, consisted of fourteen tigers killed, five tigers wounded; one panther killed, one panther wounded; two bears killed, and three bears wounded. Total, twenty-six head of "large game" killed and wounded, besides several sorts of deer.

CHAPTER XX.

FOURTH CAMPAIGN (1854)—CHANGE OF QUARTERS—RETURN TO THE OLD GROUND, BUT MEET WITH LITTLE SPORT—FIRST TIGER—INDIFFERENT SPORT—AN EXCITING CHASE—A PANIC—DANGER AND VICTORY—MY GUNS ARE STOLEN.

MY regiment, being relieved by the 21st Bombay Regiment N. I., marched from Camp Neemuch on the 9th January, 1854, and arrived at Camp Ahmedabad, in Guzerat, 244 miles distant, on the 6th February. But as I was utterly unacquainted with the peculiar language, and the country round Camp Ahmedabad, and had but such a short time to make myself familiar with either, before the hunting season commenced, I thought it best to once more visit those jungles round Camp Neemuch, of which I now had a perfect knowledge, at least over as much ground as we were permitted to hunt. To have extended our wanderings in search of "large game" beyond these particular limits, would have been hopeless, on account of the opposition we met with from the neighbouring chiefs or princes. Not a man of their subjects or dependants would have been allowed to assist us in hunting over any of their carefully preserved districts.

Postponing an intended expedition against the Guzerat lions until next year, by which time I hoped to have acquired the language of that country, at all events sufficient for sporting purposes, which is very easily done, as at most three hundred words of any dialect is a stock of knowledge large enough to make one's way at such silent work as hunting should be, I started from Camp Ahmedabad on 23rd March, for rather more than two months' shooting, and reached Camp Neemuch on 28th March. I had been assisted on my journey by the kindness of friends, who placed relays of horses, thus enabling me to easily ride the 244 miles in three days, exclusive of a stoppage of two days on the road, while my own nags went forward at "Kairwarra," an outpost about half way between the two camps. The journey was a very pleasant one, through an extremely wild part of the country, covered with vast forests and dense jungle, abounding with the most beautiful and bold scenery. My camels and servants had already reached Neemuch, having been started on the 11th March from Ahmedabad.

The party for this hunting trip consisted of Dr. R. G. Lord, 21st Regiment Bombay N. I., Lieutenants H. E. Forbes and F. Loch, 1st Bombay Lancers, and myself: afterwards to be joined, from the 1st May, by Lieutenants D. Gaye, Bombay Artillery, and Little, for the last month's sport during this "hot season."

We commenced operations on 1st April, 1854, at "Milana" village, fifteen miles from Camp, where our tents had been sent on overnight. Here we found a panther, in a thick cover of "corinda" bushes, which we burnt down, but without being able to get a shot at this brute, for he would not show or leave the thicket. He moved from one bush to another without our being able to put him out; so we were reluctantly obliged to leave him alone. On beating a cover next day at this same place, the men saw a young panther, but it never came near our positions. We then tried all the likely ground about "Panghur," but without finding any large game. A little excitement was caused by Loch, who on looking into a small cave saw a bright pair of eyes at the far end of it, but we could not tell to what animal they belonged, for none would turn out in spite of all our efforts. From "Panghur" we moved on to "Rajghur," but found no game there either, although a panther, at night, killed and carried off a favourite goat of Forbes's from the midst of our servants.

We marched twelve miles on the 7th April, to "Benchore," and beat a ravine near there, out of which a large panther was started, but I alone was able to get a shot at the brute as it bolted off. My first bullet missed, but the second shot, at a hundred and fifty yards' distance, hit the panther. There was plenty of his blood to be seen, but it soon ceased entirely, and the ground was much too stony to permit tracking the prints far. At "Naal," two miles off, while beating a hill covered with thick brushwood, near the village, a young panther passed by, but was allowed to escape in the hope that its mother would follow its steps, but she did not appear. On this day a serious accident might have happened to some of our men. Having sent them forward with the guns, as usual, to the place we were about to hunt over, while we followed on horseback, an inquisitive Rajpoot, head man of some small village, chose to handle one of our loaded guns that the beaters had placed on the ground while they stooped down to drink water at a well. The gun went off right among the men, but luckily without shooting anyone. Of course, the rascal swore he had never touched the gun lock, and that it exploded entirely of its own accord; yet, on coming up, we found the second barrel also on full cock; but these sort of accidents are common enough with "blacky," nor is there any remedy, for you are obliged to occasionally entrust them with spare loaded guns.

On 10th April, we marched to "Paat," eight miles. While following on horseback, we discovered the fresh prints of a large tiger leading into a ravine about two miles off the road. We at once agreed to beat this place, and accordingly sent round the men to one end of the cover, while we posted ourselves at different points at the other. Soon after the noise of the beating commenced, a tiger was heard to roar loudly, having been started by the men out of some dense cover, but now, unluckily, one of the beaters, a man we had brought with us from Camp, being unused to this sort of work, and perhaps a little confused at hearing the tiger's voice, set off running away from the rest of the beaters, taking the big bell with him, which made a confounded noise, and headed back the tiger, that was now coming nicely on towards us. Hearing this man's noise, with loud roars the tiger at once turned round and rushed back past the beaters, close to them. They were well together, or an accident would have occurred. We now tried to drive this tiger in the opposite direction, changing our positions, and put the men in at the other end of this large cover. Lord and Loch both got long shots at this tiger, as it bolted over a hill, and caused it to again roar loudly, but on following up its course we could find no blood, except that left on the ground by the tiger's feet which were bleeding. It was so rocky all round that these prints could not be carried on far. We returned to the tents vexed at our ill luck in losing this tiger. Nor could we find it anywhere the next day about this country.

On 12th April we tried all the likely covers about "Paal," a village a few miles distant, to which we had marched, but without success. The weather had lately been cool, with a little rain now and then. Going homewards, and wishing to discharge our rifles, we fired for fun at a hyæna that got out of a cave just in front of us. Here a sad accident happened to my rifle. It was struck, about an inch from the muzzle, by a bullet fired from behind me, which completely smashed in the barrel. An extraordinary jarring sensation was felt when this rifle was so hit while in my hands.

Our next march was to "Rajpoora," a village seven miles off; our men and guns had been sent on to "Bulderkar," a village about half way, to which we rode, knowing a good ravine in that neighbourhood. Just us we had taken up our position on a sloping bank overlooking the cover below, and before the men had begun making a noise, at the far end of the ravine, I saw a fine tiger quietly sneaking off up a small ditch that branched out of this cover, immediately opposite where we were standing. In another minute or less he would have escaped us, but on my quickly giving the alarm, our "battery" was at once opened on this tiger. At first, with much roaring, he attempted to get out of shot by rushing forward, but almost instantly returned, and came bounding past our post straight for the part of the cover we were keeping watch over. We thought the tiger meant to make a determined charge, but the beast remained quiet in the dense high green reeds and other jungle that formed the cover directly beneath us. When the men finished beating this ravine, we found this tiger dead among the rocks and reeds where we had last seen him enter. It was a very stout tiger indeed, and measured eleven feet seven and a half inches. The beaters said they had put out another tiger from this same cover, but we never saw it. We now started for our tent, which we did not reach till late at night, for we had to travel in the dark through a most hilly country, with very bad paths over most stony ground.

Next day we were joined by Mr. J. H. B. H——, 1st Bombay Lancers, who was out on leave, sporting over this country. For the following six days our ill luck pursued us; we met with no sport, although at several places fresh prints were found: the weather still continued rather too cool to ensure our killing any large game.

On the 20th of April two Bheels, whom we had sent to look for an iron loading rod, left by mistake at a position we had taken up the day before, reported to us that they had been roared at by a tiger. We again started to beat once more the same cover as we did the day before. Here a small tiger quickly turned out. We allowed him almost to pass by us before firing, for we fully expected to see his mother follow along the same path. A few shots at about forty paces distant caused the little brute to grunt as loud as he could—the noise could scarcely be called a roar, as it sounded more like a hog than a tiger. These shots rolled the little tiger down a steep hill side, where we looked for him in vain for a short time; but a few days after he was discovered dead, close by, under a stone.

Before returning to the tent we set fire to the dry grass in this cover, in the hope of finding a larger tiger, but none appeared. We went a long way ahead, and stood over a rocky precipice towards which the flames of the burning grass were spreading; for by this time the whole surrounding jungle was on fire, a high wind that was blowing having caused the dry grass to burn very rapidly. Unluckily, just as we had left this spot, our men saw a large tiger, accompanied by a smaller one, prowling about on the open level ground above the range of hills, evidently confused by the fire burning around them, and not knowing where to go. The men tried to drive these brutes towards us, but they turned off, so we never saw them. On reaching the steep precipice we heard a terrible roaring close by. This was repeated every few minutes still louder. We concluded that this uproar was the old tigress calling to the cub that we had just murdered; but it proved to be the voice of a panther that was lying in a cave about forty yards from our post. On going to the spot, the panther bounded out of the cave down the rocky sides of the high hill, and was soon out of sight in the thick cover below before we were ready to fire at it. Forbes alone got one hasty, indistinct shot, but most likely missed. The smell and smoke of the burning grass had annoyed this panther, and caused it to roar so loudly for certainly half an hour together. None of us had before met with such a case.

Early the following morning, 22nd of April, a man came to our tents to say that his buffalo had been killed by a tiger last night. Lord and myself accordingly turned out in our slippers and drawers, merely each taking a double rifle to see the "kill." There was the buffalo half eaten, plainly enough. The tiger had scaled a high, thick enclosure of thorn bushes in which the animal was secured for the night. We began following up the tiger's prints, and, at last, finding they led into the cover out of which we had the evening before started two sambur, we sent for the rest of our hunting party as well as the beaters. These soon joined us, bringing Lord's and my shooting clothes and ammunition with them. After silently trying a small thick patch of jungle far out into the open plain, we took up two separate positions over the cover into which the tiger's prints had been taken. This was a long, low hill covered with very thick thorn trees. Lord, Forbes, and H—— occupied one post, while Loch and I guarded another point.

Here we presently saw a bear scampering down a path on the hill side, about a hundred yards off. We fired three shots at this bear and made him call out lustily. Almost directly after he had passed on among the dense thorn bushes, we saw a fine tiger following quietly along the very same path. We quickly fired five shots at this beast, two of which we knew had hit, but owing to the thick jungle we could not be so sure that the other bullets had told. The tiger, with loud roars, bounded out of sight almost instantly, in the surrounding jungle. We now all joined together in a body, and began following up the prints. After going about two hundred yards, we found blood in great quantities, so the "pugging up" was easy enough.

We followed this blood for half a mile, and beat some willow covers in the bed of a river, for which the tiger had made off. The first patch of jungle was empty, but at the second a great noise from the monkeys, and peafowl swearing and screaming, told us plainly of the tiger's whereabouts. Presently we saw the tiger looking half out of the thick willow bushes to see if the coast was clear, before making a bolt across an open plain for the hills beyond. Three shots were quickly fired at the beast, when it sprang back into the thicket. Again it appeared in another direction, where it tried to escape from; but three more shots once more sent it back into this dense patch of willow bushes.

We now thought it best to stop the beating, lest any of the men should be hurt by this tiger in the cover, for it would not be likely to make another attempt to escape, having been so wounded each time it exposed itself. Having formed a procession, as usual, we advanced into the cover, and soon spied the tiger lying down among some dead leaves and bushes, in which it was almost hid as it crouched down. We now formed line and fired a volley by word of command, whereupon the tiger instantly sprang up, and with terrific roars came charging down, tail up and claws out, straight for where we were standing, about twenty or thirty paces off.

Here a most laughable panic occurred; such a hasty retreat took place that at least a dozen hunters and Bheels were all rolling in a heap, one on the top of the other, on the ground. This was chiefly owing to the smoke from our guns having hung in a thick cloud before us on firing this last volley; for there was not a breath of wind in this high, dark cover to blow away the smoke. Thus, not being able to see clearly what was happening, each man concluded the tiger was in the very midst of us. All that was plainly visible was the tiger's tail stuck upright in the air over the cloud of smoke as he rushed on us with most appalling roars. I was the only one of the whole party who was enabled to fire my second barrel, the bullet of which most fortunately dropped the tiger dead at our feet, striking the beast somewhere in the face. Very many bruises and scratches were received in this fight. One man had stamped on Lord's face in his efforts to escape. No one knew how the panic had originated, but all blamed each other. There is no accounting for these little accidents, for they occur and are over in a moment. We returned to our tents with the game, which proved to be a fine tigress nine feet two inches long. This tigress the Bheels declared, from certain marks, to be the one that had recently killed two men.

We had turned out and bagged our game this morning before breakfast, after a nine hours' chase, so were dreadfully hungry. The bear we did not look for again, nor count as wounded, for no blood could be found on the spot; but there is little doubt that he also was hit.

Next day, 23rd April, we moved on to "Kungaira" village, where Forbes and H—— did not arrive till long after dark, having lost their road.

On the 24th, we had directed the baggage to be sent on to "Buddana," ten miles, when a man reported that some bullocks had lately been destroyed by tigers at "Palasirree" village, six miles in the opposite direction. We agreed to hunt there, and ride afterwards on to our tents in the evening. Unluckily at this place we could get no proper sort of men to help us, for no Bheels lived here, so we had to collect a parcel of useless fellows, accustomed only to tending cattle and working in the fields, in whose courage not the slightest confidence could be placed. On arriving at the ravine in which the tiger was said to live, we took up our position on a high rocky ledge overlooking the dense cover below, which was formed of an almost impenetrable tangled mass of "corinda" bushes, high grass, and thorn-trees. Presently the noise of the beaters was heard, when two young tigers, about half-grown, rushed out of a cave opposite where we were standing, and made direct for the thick cover the men were now beating. As they raced past us we fired, and evidently wounded these youngsters, for they roared as loud as they were able. Just now, above all the din of the beaters, was heard the voice of a large tiger. It afterwards appeared that on the men nearing the part of the cover in which this brute was lying, he began roaring at them, whereupon most of the beaters took to their legs, and ran off out of the jungle; our own men being now alone, were obliged to also follow them, and in the hurry dropped a powder-horn, with which they loaded the pistols for blank shots while beating. After calling out to each other, our men told us what had happened; so, as the wind was blowing in that direction, we changed our ground to the other end of the cover, and sent the beaters round to where we had first posted ourselves, directing them to set fire to the high grass. This they at once did, willingly enough, for it saved them all further bother or risk in beating this cover. Unfortunately, just as we had left this part of the ground, the men all saw a very large tiger get up out of the high dry grass and walk off across an open plain, having been disturbed by the fire, which turned him away from our new position. The men described him as being of a tremendous size, and almost free from stripes, so he must have been a very old tiger indeed.

The burning grass now caused us to again shift our ground for a minute or two, until the fire had passed on. Just as we regained this last post, we saw a tiger coming on about twenty yards off, on a sloping bank a little below. He at once was well "peppered," but managed to hide himself in the dense "corinda" bushes. We now, taking our two huntsmen, went down into the cover, and began looking about for the powder-horn they said had been dropped. While thus scattered about, searching among the dead leaves, &c., a terrible roar was heard about six or seven yards only distant. It appeared that H——, who was a mere spectator of this sport, and had no gun even with him at the time, had approached a thick "corinda" bush, in which a large tigress was lying hid. She at once sprang out at him with fearful roars, but most luckily seemed somehow to be stopped or caught by the strong branches off the bush, in which she struggled hard to get at H——. But these boughs are very tough, and fortunately for him did not break or give way. H—— at once threw himself down flat, while we, on hastily looking round, saw directly what had happened, and as quick as possible fired six shots over H—— at the tigress while thus stuck in the middle of this bush. Whereupon the beast bounced out of the back part of the large thick "corinda," and sprang at a bound into the dense mass of tangled brushwood that formed the centre and thickest part of this cover. There was no panic this time, but we left H—— outside the jungle, which was on fire all round, and stifling hot, while we at once set about finding this tigress. After cautiously going a little distance, keeping a bright look out under every bush, I at last viewed her, lying very close under a very thick "corinda," near which the fire was now burning. For some time we vainly tried to get a shot at this brute. At last we thus managed to fire on her at about ten paces distance. Loch and myself, by lying down side by side on the ground, could just get an indistinct sight of the tigress. Lord and Forbes, with the rest of the men, kept guard over us. On firing, the beast, with loud roars, jumped up, but we directly floored her again with more shots. Our "band" or drums all the while made a terrific row just behind us to prevent her charging in that direction. We drew out the body, and skinned her under some trees a little way off, and then mounted our horses and prepared to ride straight across a very broken country for "Buddana" village, fourteen miles distant.

We discharged all our guns to prevent accidents, before entrusting them to the beaters. These men, as usual, were directed to follow as far as they could before night came on, then to sleep during the night at some village or town on the way, and follow on to our camp at daylight next morning. Before leaving, I supplied my servants with money to hire watchmen, as is the custom in this part of the country, to guard any property while the owners sleep at any place they may be travelling past for the night. While riding towards our tent, Loch suddenly felt so unwell, that he could not keep his saddle. With some difficulty we procured men at a village about half way, and had him carried on a cot on their shoulders to our camp. The road was so stony, and lay through such thick jungle, where branches overhanging the path often required to be cut down before we could proceed, that we did not reach our tents till near midnight, travelling very slowly by torchlight, for the night was pitch dark. We had started to hunt to-day at 8 A.M., so had a long day's work on a very hot day, without any food; this, added to the heat of the fire and a bad sprain, caused by a fall over some rocks, had upset poor Loch. Here we half expected to meet Lieutenant Little and Lieutenant D. Gaye from camp, but were disappointed.

Early next morning the skin of the tigress reached us; but we were horrified to hear that three of our guns left in charge of the beaters overnight had been stolen, while our servants and the men with them were sleeping at the village of "Gidwarra," a place they had stopped at when night overtook them. Lord, Forbes, and self, at once rode to the place, where we discovered that the three stolen guns all belonged to me, or were in my charge. I was the only one of the whole party that had ever before hunted over this country, so that stealing my guns only out of a pile of thirteen double guns, clearly showed malice or spite on the part of the thieves. These rogues had no doubt been directed to commit this robbery at the suggestion of some more influential villain or other, who disapproved of our visiting this neighbourhood for sporting purposes. This was a loss of 100*l*. This impudent robbery was committed by the very watchmen supplied by the chief man of the village of "Gidwarra," to guard our guns while our servants slept, and with his connivance, for he indirectly admitted as much to us. Our people being quite tired out after such a hard day's work, of course could not be expected to guard the guns. The only wonder is that robberies of this description are not more frequent in this particular part of the country, considering the perfect impunity with which they can be committed, always provided that the loser is not a person of any authority.

CHAPTER XXI.

H—— RETURNS TO CAMP—KILL A HUGE TIGER—AN IMPUDENT PANTHER—A MAD DOG—MEET THREE TIGERS—KILL TWO—MORE GOOD SPORT.

OUR party was now reduced to three; for Mr. H—— returned to camp satiated with tiger-hunting, and Loch was too lame to share in the sport. Therefore, Forbes, Lord, and myself, went to hunt in the "Koondia" ravine. Soon after the beating began, a fine tigress passed within thirty yards of the rock on which we were standing. She was severely wounded, and with a roar sprang out of sight into some dense jungle just in her front. Shortly after, she again was seen for a moment by Lord in some long grass. He once more made her roar, and retreated into the thick cover. The men now came up, so, each taking two rifles, we ran a long way ahead, hoping to get another shot at this tigress should the beaters be able to again drive her past our position, which was on a rocky bank overlooking an open space where the grass had lately been burnt. Here, to our delight, on the noise of the Bheels being once more heard, we soon saw an immense tiger slowly trotting straight towards us. We allowed him to come within about thirty paces before firing. This tiger dropped at once at the first shot or two, and could not again rise, or move away, for his back was broken about the middle of his body. His hind quarters seemed perfectly paralyzed; but he could move round in a circle with the help of his fore-arms, which he continued doing, clawing and biting at every tree, bush, and large stone within his reach, roaring at us every now and then. Seeing he could not escape, for fun, Lord and myself began pelting the tiger with large stones, at which he roared still louder; but for this conduct we were very properly reproved by Forbes, who lectured us on thus insulting a fallen foe. The men had now finished beating the jungle, and approached our rock, not being aware that we had shot this tiger. Before coming up, they had set fire to a patch of thick high grass, expecting the wounded tigress might be hiding there. Directly this large tiger saw the smoke ascend, he cocked his ears, and made frantic efforts to escape. This proves how much these animals dread fire, and how well they know what seeing the jungle burning means. Perhaps they are sometimes rather puzzled to escape when the grass has been set on fire at many different points, and continues to burn fiercely on all the hills around, as will sometimes happen.

We now descended the rocky bank, and walking up within a pace or two of the wounded tiger's reach, put him out of his misery by a ball through his brain. This was the largest tiger any of us had yet seen. He measured twelve feet seven and a half inches long, and was stout in proportion—a perfect monster.

For the next three days, we had no sport, but were then joined at "Goolambah" village, to which place we had marched, after beating the covers near the river "Chumbul," by Little and D. Gaye, who had ridden on from camp and followed us on from our last halting-place to this spot. While at dinner, in our tent, after dark, the next day, a great uproar was suddenly heard, which arose from a panther, actually having the impudence to carry off Dr. Lord's poor little dog "Tim," that was at the time in the same tent with us, or close by it. The dog's cries, as the panther took him off, past all our servants, who were scattered about, gave us the first intimation of what had occurred. Instantly an alarm was raised, while we hastened after the panther, firing shots in the air to frighten him. Other men quickly followed, with lighted sticks and lanthorns. We all made the utmost noise. The night was very dark, and the jungle, through which the dog was walked off, was very dense and thorny, with large pieces of rock scattered over the ground. Many bruises and scratches occurred to us all, for we merely had on slippers and drawers at the time. At length, after going about 400 yards, we recovered the body of the dog, which the panther had dropped, on being so hotly pursued. Poor Tim was quite dead, having received a blow of the panther's paw. Next morning, we erected a cairn to his memory, for he was a great pet, and tried hard to turn out the panther from some deep caves to which we tracked him, but it was not possible.

The tents were now sent on to "Indoreghur" ravine, eight miles, while we beat along the hill's side. After firing at some herds of cheetul, and a few sambur that were started, we heard the loud roars of a tiger that had turned out of a cave at the foot of the high rocky range of hills on which we were walking. Loch, now recovered, only got a good shot at this tiger, for the rest of us had passed on, but many other bullets were sent after the brute, as it galloped off in the plain below, roaring loudly. Here the dense jungle soon hid it from our view.

We tried hard to follow up this tiger's prints, but the ground was too stony; nor could we find any blood, so do not consider this tiger wounded, although Loch was only about thirty yards off when he fired, and made this beast roar as if hit.

On the next day we most carefully looked over the whole of the famous "Ramboon" cover, where, last year, five tigers and a bear were discovered, but this time it was empty. At night there was another disturbance in our camp. We concluded from the roaring noise which awoke us about midnight, that a tiger had seized a horse, or some such catastrophe, at least; but it turned out, after all, to be only two camels fighting!

While quietly drinking tea in the tent, all being very lightly clad indeed, a mad dog rushed in and pinned Dr. Lord's remaining pet dog, "Jack." Great was the confusion; everybody trying to gain the top of the table, or some safe place, out of the mangy cur's way. Four rifle-shots were fired into this mad dog before he died. These guns were in the tent, and were fired in the hurry, regardless of the many men, horses, cattle, camels, &c., all round us. Most luckily nobody was hurt by the bullets, as they whizzed off the rocky ground on all sides.

Again tried "Ramkoon," for it was hard to believe that this lovely cover was blank, but nothing was seen. We ordered a move on to "Sawunt" village, seven miles. Here we beat all the likely ravines and covers round the fort of "Hinglazghur." Just as we had taken up our first position, a very fine buck sambur, with wide antlers, got up out of some high grass. Thinking no tiger could be in this cover, from this circumstance, we fired at the sambur and hit him, at about 200 yards' distance. Then followed up his blood for half-a-mile, but lost the stag after all. While next proceeding to beat the rocky side of a steep hill here, covered with thick jungle and high brushwood, we saw two cowherds up trees. These men told us they had just seen a tiger while tending their cattle, and had climbed these trees for safety. We quickly divided, and took up five separate positions along the side of this hill, being each about fifty yards apart, so that no animal could pass unseen by us. The men were sent back a long way, with orders to beat towards our posts. Soon after, three tigers were seen quietly approaching, one was killed dead, and the other two both badly wounded. We now followed up the blood, of which there was plenty, and soon found another tiger dead; but this we did not know to be the case until a brace of bullets had been fired into the already dead tiger, only a small part of whose skin could be seen in the thick bushes under which it had died. All the precautions, as if about to attack a live tiger, were gone through,—such as sending the men to the rear—placing the guns ready at our feet, and forming a line for a rapid file firing. The remaining tiger we lost, after taking his prints and blood some little distance on, for it was getting late, and we had to skin the two tigers on the ground. It would have been impossible to carry them over such hilly country. The tigress measured ten feet five inches; the young tiger, nine feet four inches.

On the following day, 7th May, our hunting party rode over to beat "Chutterbooj" ravine, four miles off. Here they found fresh prints of two large tigers, but could not discover the brutes themselves. I, with two Bheels, tried to follow up the third wounded tiger, shot yesterday. With much difficulty we carried the prints and blood on for about 300 yards further, through dreadfully thick jungle, but lost them here, on the ground becoming too stony. Small tufts of hair, where this tiger had fallen and scraped itself over large rocks, were visible about, so it was sure to die. I also followed up a bear's prints, but failed to find him. The weather was very cool all day, with thunder and lightning, and much rain.

We sent the men and guns on early to "Soorlea," three miles. This little village, on our arrival, was in a state of excitement, some robbers having stolen some cattle there last night. Our next consideration was, how to effectually beat the immense ravine named "Noorsinghur," where a large tiger escaped me last year. This time we thought it best to drive the wide cover another way, so took up six separate positions, right across the entrance of the ravine, covering at least half a mile of ground. The beaters were told off into three sets of men: these presently advanced parallel to each other, in famous style, and beat the whole cover, at least one and a half miles long, beautifully, but no large game whatever appeared.

In the morning of the 9th, before breakfast, Dr. Lord and

Mr. Little caught, with their rods, upwards of fifty "murrel" fish in the small lake there. We sent the baggage on to "Ranee ka Roree" village, eleven miles, while we started early with our gun carriers for "Dowd" village. There we breakfasted under a shady tree, while more Bheels were being assembled, and then proceeded to beat "Chutturbooj" ravine. We started, and instantly killed an old bear. After skinning the bear on the spot where he fell, we went a long way up the ravine, thinking that any other beast in the neighbourhood would have been disturbed by our shots. Unluckily, on the beating recommencing, two tigers were put out of a cave close by where we had just killed the bear. These tigers left the big ravine without ever coming near our position. While the men were thus beating this ravine, we were kept in a great state of excitement, by hearing our men fire double pistol shots, the signal for a tiger being on foot. We tried hard to follow up the prints of these tigers, but the ground was too stony. From the direction they were going, it seemed likely that we should find them in "Ambah" cover, four miles off, across a perfectly open plain. We walked there, and beat that place also, but without success.

On the 10th, we determined to have another search for the tigers that escaped us yesterday. First of all we went to try "Ambah" cover once more, but agreed to beat it in a different direction. Soon afterwards a great noise of monkeys and peafowl was heard; and a tigress now appeared, but stopped short in a thick bush just opposite the bank on which we were standing. A fine tiger also broke cover; this brute I rolled over with the first ball. This shot startled the tigress, and caused her to rush out in the plain at a great pace. She was fired at by three other guns of our party. The tiger quickly picked himself up, and bolted back into the thick cover. By this time the Bheels had come up, having left off beating on hearing our shots. One of these men was placed up a tree on the look-out, lest the tiger should attempt to make off, while with the rest of the men we began following up the prints of the tigress. Strange to say, no blood could be found. The ground all round was chiefly composed of sheet rock, that is, smooth level slabs of rock resembling pavement. It was, therefore, next to impossible to follow up the prints over this hard flat surface. After beating rather an open part of this ravine—a mere continuation of the cover with very little jungle in it, but without being able to again find the tigress—we all returned to where the Bheel had been left up the high tree on the watch over the tiger. This man pointed out the very bush in which the wounded tiger was now lying, for, as we had expected, on finding the place quite quiet, the tiger had endeavoured to escape from the cover altogether, no doubt fancying that his enemies had left the place; but he was soon headed back by the man up the tree calling out at him. After firing several shots at guess, and throwing volleys of large stones into the bush, the tiger suddenly jumped up, and with roars rushed back into a still thicker part of this cover, getting a shot or two from us as he passed by. In vain we tried to stone the brute out of this patch of jungle. I happened to cross over to the other side of the cover, and here saw the tiger crouching down among some high grass on the edge of the thicket. Quietly calling the rest of our party, we fired a volley into him at about forty paces off. This upset the tiger, but he managed to spring back into the dense high green reeds and dry grass close by, where we could no longer see him. Climbing up high trees all round, at length the long grass was in one particular spot seen to quiver slightly. This betrayed the tiger's presence; for the heaving of his sides as he lay panting had caused this tremulous motion of the grass. A shot, fired into this spot, started the tiger with loud roars, and he was again saluted by three guns while crossing a rather open space in the ravine for a still denser patch of willow bushes lower down the long cover. We followed the brute, and got a few indistinct shots now and then as it moved off through the thick bushes. On going round to the opposite side of the ravine, the tiger could now be clearly seen lying under a large "corinda," seeming very much done. A few more bullets fired here killed it outright.

We were now recalled by our men, whom we had directed to climb up trees for safety while we alone followed up this just killed tiger, to the furthest end of this long ravine, down the whole length of which we had been chasing our last victim. They assured us that a tiger had just been roaring in the thick jungle, over which they were watching. We set fire to this place, and waited patiently, silently guarding different points around until the high grass and bushes, in which the tiger was supposed to be hiding, were nearly burnt down by the fire. No animal appeared; and as it was now getting dark, we returned to skin the last killed tiger, which, greatly to our astonishment, turned out after all to be only a tigress. This was a very large stout beast, and measured eleven feet and a half. From the extraordinary amount of trouble she gave us before being killed, as well as from its great size, we all thought it must be a male tiger. We took this beast's skin off by the light of the moon, which was shining brightly, and returned to our tents very late, quite tired out with such a long day's work. The tiger last heard to roar by our men no doubt was the first wounded tigress that had returned for its companion.

CHAPTER XXII.

Smart encounters—Lose a very fine tiger—Stung by a scorpion—The bag—Return to Ahmedabad.

For two days our extraordinary good fortune forsook us, but when we reached Bhysrode fort it returned; for here, after searching the whole of "Andara" cover, at the very end of it, a fine tiger bolted out past Little and Loch's post. Loch fired two shots as the brute galloped off, but did not feel at all sure that he had hit him. This caused the tiger to rush back into the thick jungle again past Forbes' and my post. Forbes fired one shot, but could not clearly see the tiger as it raced through the dense bushes. I was unable to fire at all, as he moved by my front.

Now, another disturbance and more shots were heard. This was caused by Loch firing at an old bear, that attempted to break at the very same part of the cover. The bear rushed back into the cover, past Forbes, who also fired at the brute, whereupon the bear turned round, and made for the slight low tree up which Forbes was posted, who firmly believed the bear was about to visit him. But I now got two shots at the bear from my post, and luckily killed him.

With all the beaters we now followed up the prints of the wounded tiger. After going about a hundred yards, we found three specks of blood. We formed the men up into still closer order, and, making the "band" strike up, we advanced through the high dense cover, throwing innumerable stones on all sides Presently, a Bheel, sent up to look out from each high tree we passed, saw the tiger lying down a few yards in front. A shot fired to make sure, showed he was quite dead. This was a splendid tiger, in full vigour and "plumage," measuring twelve feet six inches and three-quarters long.

We next tried another patch of willow bushes, about a mile up this ravine, but found no more game. The dead bear was carried home on a camel, sent for the purpose from our tents. Rain now fell, so we walked on to our little camp.

For the next four days we met with no sport, unless some murrel fish, three feet long, caught by Lord, can be so considered; or unless the confusion caused by an onslaught of bees, whereby, as usual, my head was much swollen up, may be deemed sport!

We had now moved on to "Janodeep" village. While beating the beautiful cover called "Goodalee," two young tigresses, nearly full grown, turned out and were quickly killed by our shots. We took off their coats, under some shady trees close by; they measured nine feet four inches and half, and nine feet two inches long respectively.

The following day was a blank one, but on the next, the 20th of May, while beating "Putloee" ravine, in the plains below the range of hills over which we had lately been hunting, a fine tigress was found. Here Forbes fired rather too soon, which caused the beast to retreat back into the thickest part of this good cover of high willow trees and bushes, with much long grass and green reeds. We had the greatest trouble to discover whereabouts in the thick jungle this tigress had hidden herself. After firing very many shots at guess, and flinging volleys of large stones into every possible part of the cover, but without being able to make the tigress show, we crossed over to the other bank of this deep ravine, leaving Gaye to look out, while we went round above the end of the cover. All being quiet, the tigress began to move, when D. Gaye fired several shots at the brute. By this time we had got round opposite the place where this tiger was concealed. Gaye's bullets made the beast roar, but we could not even now see her. Some of these balls, as they rebounded off the hard rocky ground, whizzed most unpleasantly close past our heads, and compelled us to beg him to cease firing. We now all went down in a body into the cover, and found the tigress dead under the hollow roots and stump of a large dead tree, where she had been protected from many of our bullets. This tigress measured eleven feet and an inch or two.

We beat a long hill-side, covered with high thorn bushes, near "Kookee" ravine, at "Limree," on the 21st of May. Here a bear was shot dead on attempting to pass our post. In doing this, a lighted greased patch from Lord's rifle set fire to the high grass around, and as there was a high wind at the time, we had much trouble in extinguishing this burning grass, which would soon have spread over hill and dale, spoiling all chance of further sport, by driving every sort of wild beast out of the country. A herd of about twenty-five sambur passed the beaters, but we did not get a shot at these stags. We skinned the bear, and then beat "Kokee" cover, but found it was empty.

On the 22nd we marched seven miles, on to "Morwun" village, and beat the extreme end of "Kokee" ravine, in which some men were engaged in cutting down trees. Nevertheless, an immense tiger was put out of this cover, but the brute passed over a steep bank leading out of the ravine, without being seen at all by us. The beaters viewed him and gave the alarm, but we could not again find this fine tiger in any of the other patches of jungle around in which we looked for him. This tiger had been lying within only a few yards of where these wood-cutters were at work, which proves how little these brutes fear men in this country. His footprints were larger than any we had yet seen.

Next morning we again went to the same cover to look for yesterday's tiger, and beat it as before. Forbes and self agreed to watch the path by which this large tiger had yesterday escaped out of this ravine. The beating began when the men saw this monster tiger climb over the steep hill out of the thick cover below, at the very same place he had done the day before. To our intense annoyance Forbes and I discovered that we had mistaken the exact path over which we were to have kept guard. The tiger passed clear, only a few yards beyond where we were lying down on some rocks without our being able to even see him. As before, the tiger could not be again found anywhere, although we hunted many places for a long way all round the neighbourhood. The rest of our hunting party were posted at separate points of the cover out of which this tiger broke, but never saw him either. Cruel disappointment this! Returned home rather late, quite depressed at losing such a magnificent tiger. The beaters described his size as being something wonderful, which report his tremendous prints fully carried out.

Next day, after shooting many large fish in the river, we moved on to Deypoora. Here we killed a large bear in a rocky ravine far out in the plains. This bear growled at our men and refused to stir, so we were called by them to shoot him in a cave in which he had sought refuge. On skinning the bear his body was found to be one mass of bruises, this, no doubt, as the Bheels suggested, had been caused by his accidentally falling from some high tree up which he had climbed after honey or fruit, either by slipping or perhaps a bough breaking with his weight.

The loss of the big tiger at the upper end of "Kokee" still haunted us, so we once more walked over to that cover a long way off, and again beat it, taking extraordinary precaution to guard every inch of ground. But the tiger was not at home, so we sorrowfully retraced our steps homeward. He had given us two chances and we had not much right to complain.

The next three days afforded no sport, although we tried many likely covers each day. In one of these places, while waiting in ambush for any game that might be disturbed, a scorpion stung me, even through my thick leather belts, but the pain was so great, that my arm and shoulder were much swollen, and useless for some hours.

On the 29th of May, having sent on our camels and baggage to "Panghur" fort, while beating "Bahara" ravine for the last time, the men put out a tigress, which was killed dead, the very moment it showed itself, by a single bullet. This animal measured ten feet seven and a half inches long. On the 30th of May, we walked four miles over the high hills here, to "Soorlee" village, where many bullocks were said to have been lately killed. While beating a steep hill side here, covered with low jungle, a panther was seen, but out of shot. We tried, by running ahead, to get another view of this panther, but failed. This was our last day's hunting, as our leave of absence was so nearly expired that we had but time to get back to Camp Neemuch on the following morning, after cleaning and packing up the "battery."

The "bag," during this two months' hunting expedition, was,—thirteen tigers killed, five tigers wounded; one panther wounded; four bears killed, and one bear wounded; besides many deer of different sorts killed and wounded. Total, large game killed and wounded, twenty-four head.

Game is getting very scarce in this part of "Rajpootana." On returning to Camp Neemuch, having, by the kindness of friends, several horses and camels at different stages, placed for us along the road, Little and myself rode back to Camp Ahmedabad, 244 miles, in three days. We slept out at night under trees, by our horses, and resumed our journey next morning, till dark. We got back just in time; for the "monsoon," or rainy season, set in heavily directly afterwards.

THE END.